Chairwork
Theory and Practice

Remco van der Wijngaart

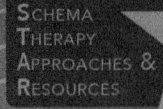

Chairwork: Theory and Practice

English translation of *Stoelentechniek: theorie en praktijk*

© Pavilion Publishing & Media

The author has asserted his rights in accordance with the Copyright, Designs and Patents Act (1988) to be identified as the author of this work.

Published by:
Pavilion Publishing and Media Ltd
Blue Sky Offices, 25 Cecil Pashley Way
Shoreham by Sea, West Sussex
BN43 5FF

Tel: 01273 434 943
Email: info@pavpub.com
Web: www.pavpub.com

Published 2021

All rights reserved. No part of this publication may be reproduced, stored in a retrieval system, or transmitted in any form or by any means, electronic, mechanical, photocopying, recording or otherwise, without prior permission in writing of the publisher and the copyright owners.

A catalogue record for this book is available from the British Library.

ISBN: 978-1-803882-38-3

Pavilion Publishing and Media is a leading publisher of books, training materials and digital content in mental health, social care and allied fields. Pavilion and its imprints offer must-have knowledge and innovative learning solutions underpinned by sound research and professional values.

First published in Dutch under the title *Stoelentechniek: theorie en praktijk* by Remco van der Wijngaart, edition: 1
Copyright © Bohn Stafleu van Loghum is een imprint van Springer Media B.V., onderdeel van Springer Nature, 2022
This edition has been translated and published under licence from Springer Media B.V., part of Springer Nature. Springer Media B.V., part of Springer Nature takes no responsibility and shall not be made liable for the accuracy of the translation.

Author: Remco van der Wijngaart
Cover design: Emma Dawe, Pavilion Publishing and Media Ltd
Page layout and typesetting: Anthony Pitt, Pavilion Publishing and Media Ltd
Printing: CPI Antony Rowe

Contents

Chairwork: Theory and Practice ii

Acknowledgements 1

About the author 3

Foreword 5

Chapter 1: Introduction 7

Chapter 2: The analysis phase 37

Chapter 3: The initial phase of therapy 61

Chapter 4: The middle phase of therapy 97

Chapter 5: The final phase of therapy 125

Chapter 6: Pitfalls for therapists 145

Chapter 7: Specialist areas of application 157

Chapter 8: Chairwork online 185

References 197

Acknowledgements

The work is done, and the manuscript is finished. This is the moment to look back, not only at the content but also at the people who helped make it possible to write this book. First of all, I would like to thank BSL publishers, and in particular Yulma Perk and Hester Presburg. Yulma, your enthusiasm, kindness and encouragement were a tremendous help for me to take on this project and to keep going. Hester, once again I have been impressed by your prompt, effective and practical support throughout this whole journey.

I'm glad to have a platform with this acknowledgement to thank Julie Krans. Julie, when we agreed that you would take on the scientific research for this book, neither of us realised how much work that would involve. You have succeeded in bringing clarity to this wilderness with your contribution to Chapter 1. I experienced your qualities as a person again in this professional collaboration: you're always ready to help and discuss ideas, picking out every inconsistency in the text with your sharp eye and scientific mind, and supporting the writing process with your humour, warmth and clear mind. I am happy and grateful to know you, and happy and grateful for our collaboration on this book!

Hélène Bögels, I was always impressed by how quickly you read through chapters and gave feedback on these texts with a wonderfully expert and positive attitude. Over the past years, you have not only shown yourself to be a great teacher and therapist, but also to be a very good book editor. You are also a warm and friendly person and I am very happy with our collaboration over the past years, and during the writing of this book!

I am very grateful to Hannie van Genderen for writing the excellent Foreword and for providing feedback on the writing. Hannie, working together on writing this book is a new step in our close collaboration that began in 1995. I have always found this collaboration in teaching, intervision, workshops and presentations to be enriching and instructive. This was also true of this collaboration, thank you!

I would also like to mention Matthew Pugh, author of several articles on chairwork and of the book Cognitive Behavioural Chairwork. Matthew, thank you for selflessly sharing your articles and the teaching materials you have developed over the years. I would also like to thank the many students and clients with whom I have done countless chair exercises over the past twenty-six years. Thank you for your willingness to be open to this technique. Your feedback on the experiences brought about by the exercises made an essential contribution to the development of this book. Thank you!

Finally, I want to thank my children Robin and Arthur, simply for who they are and the joy they give to life.

About the author

 **Remco van der Wijngaart** works as a psychotherapist in private practice in Maastricht, the Netherlands. Initially trained in CBT, he was trained and supervised in Schema Therapy personally by Dr Jeffrey Young from 1996 until 2000. Remco specializes in borderline patients, patients with cluster C personality disorders and anxiety and depressive disorders.

As a director of the Dutch Institute for Schema Therapy (in the Netherlands known as Van Genderen Opleidingen), Remco organizes training courses and workshops in the field of schema therapy. More than 6,700 therapists have participated in these courses. He produced and directed several audio-visual productions, including *Schema therapy, step by step* and *Schema therapy for the Avoidant-, Dependent- and Obsessive-Compulsive Personality Disorder.* He is the author of the book *Imagery Rescripting, theory and practice* (2021).

Foreword

Within schema therapy, experiential techniques are essential for bringing about change in persistent patterns of thinking and behaviour. Chairwork is one of the most widely used experiential techniques, partly because it can be applied relatively easily at any phase of therapy.

However, chairwork can be confusing if the therapist does not have a clear picture of which of the client's sides or modes are in which chair. It is very useful to have a book that explains this – yet writing a book on chairwork is no simple matter, because by definition the technique is an exercise in three-dimensional space where the position of the chair is not arbitrary, but has a different meaning in each type of exercise. In this book, Remco van der Wijngaart explains this clearly. The examples based on two running case studies also help the therapist to develop a 'language' that can be used to speak to a client's different sides.

The author explores why therapists must understand that different phases of therapy require the chair technique to be applied differently. He also considers why it is important for therapists to realise that they may encounter pitfalls, partly due to their own schemas, when they apply the chair technique. The book devotes extensive attention to what these pitfalls may be, and to how the therapist can address them (with or without the help of chairs). Later chapters explain how chairwork can also be used in a modified form in partner relationship therapy, in groups and as a supplementary technique in more symptom-oriented treatments. The final chapter on online treatment is very worthwhile, not only in times of pandemics, but also in a world where therapy is increasingly provided remotely.

Role-playing is a well-known component of cognitive behavioural therapy, but chairwork's greater level of detail is a welcome addition to this. The technique is particularly useful when there are persistent survival strategies that hinder the progress of therapy. In short, this book will give therapists a clear and comprehensive overview of the possibilities of applying chairwork in various settings and for various problems.

Hannie van Genderen

Chapter 1: Introduction

Chapter 1: Introduction

Written by Julie Krans* and Remco van der Wiijngaart

*   Julie Krans is an assistant professor in clinical psychology at Radboud University Nijmegen, and senior researcher at Pro Persona Overwaal centre for anxiety, OCD, and PTSD. Her research focuses on imagery rescripting and schema therapy for chronic psychological disorders.

Chapter map	
1.1	Introduction
1.2	What is chairwork?
1.3	A history of chairwork
1.4	Forms of chairwork
1.5	Scientific research on chairwork
1.6	Research into the effectiveness of chairwork
1.7	Research into the experiences of clients and therapists with chairwork
1.8	Chairwork in schema therapy – the basis of this book
1.9	Chapter summary
1.10	Case studies in this book

1.1 Introduction

Welcome to this book on chairwork, a technique that has been used for decades in various schools of therapy including gestalt therapy, cognitive behavioural therapy and emotion-focused therapy. In this introductory chapter, we will explore what chairwork is and how it can be used to help create strong corrective emotional experiences. We will also examine how the technique has developed over time, and what different forms are used in contemporary clinical practice.

After an overview of the ways in which chairwork is used across different therapeutic frameworks, the rest of the book describes the technique as it is used in schema therapy. For readers who are unfamiliar with schema therapy, this chapter also gives an overview of its core elements and the place that chairwork occupies in its different phases of treatment. Finally, there is an overview of research evidence on how the technique works, and how therapists and clients experience it.

1.2 What is chairwork?

Chairwork, or the chair technique, refers to emotion-focused interventions in which chairs are used in a therapeutic setting to represent the client's thoughts, feelings, symptoms or different aspects of their personality, as well as significant others or problems in their life. While sitting in a chair, clients express their thoughts and feelings, possibly inhabiting one aspect of themselves or a significant other person. Then, by getting up from the chair and looking back at it from some physical distance, clients can experience an emotional distance from those things the chair has now come to represent. This emotional distance creates space for the client to have more insight into their symptoms or difficulties, and it also opens a dialogue with these issues, people or problems. The possibilities of chairwork make it a useful technique in a variety of therapeutic contexts including CBT (Pugh, 2017) and emotion-focused therapy (Greenberg et al., 1993).

1.3 A history of chairwork

The following description and history of chairwork is in no way exhaustive, but is primarily intended to show that chairwork has long been used in various therapeutic movements and, as an intervention, is not tied to any one of them. For a more detailed description of the development of the chair technique, please refer to books by Kellogg (2015) and Pugh (2020).

1.3.1 Psychodrama

Chairwork was originally developed by Jacob Moreno (1889-1974), the pioneer of psychodrama and group psychotherapy, to externalise parts of the client's internal world. In his group exercises, Moreno used chairs to make it possible to see and hear a client's internal dialogue (Moreno, 2014), and group members then interpreted the different aspects of this dialogue from different chairs.

1.3.2 Gestalt therapy

Fritz Perls (1893-1970) attended Moreno's psychodrama sessions and became familiar with the chair technique, to which he then gave a central role in his Gestalt therapy. He developed a 'two-chair technique' in which two sides of the client, for example the critical and the criticised sides, entered into a dialogue with each other. But he also used the 'empty-chair technique' to have clients talk to absent others, including deceased loved ones. Perls had the client play all the roles on the different chairs, and under his influence the chair technique became more suitable for individual therapy.

1.3.3 Behavioural therapy

One of the first applications of the chairwork to change specific behaviour patterns was as part of roleplay for assertiveness training. Joseph Wolpe (1915-1997) regularly used 'psychodramas' during his sessions, which were later used widely in behavioural therapy as skills training (behavioural rehearsal). In this context, the chair technique was a way to have clients practice new, desired behaviours in simulated situations from their own lives.

1.3.4 Rational emotive behaviour therapy

The principle of rational emotive behaviour therapy (REBT) is that symptoms are caused by irrational thoughts. The aim of REBT is therefore to arrive at more rational premises. However, some clients prove resistant to change, and for these situations Albert Ellis (1913-2007) recommended a variation of chairwork to bring irrational and rational thoughts into sharper focus. For example, thoughts of irrational fear might be 'seated' in one chair with rational counter-arguments 'seated' in another.

1.3.5 Cognitive therapy

Although the key principle of the cognitive therapy developed by Aaron T Beck (1921-2021) is that change can be brought about through cognitive interventions, Beck was also open to other approaches as long as they were compatible with the principles of the model. He saw experiential interventions such as chairwork as particularly effective methods of bringing about cognitive change (Beck et al., 1985). In fact, chairwork is often recommended when more 'traditional' cognitive interventions prove insufficiently effective (Beck, 1995).

1.3.6 Third wave cognitive behavioural therapies

Although they differ greatly from each other, therapy models such as compassion-focused therapy (CFT) and dialectical behaviour therapy (DBT) also share some important characteristics, such as the therapeutic importance of acceptance, non-judgmental awareness and metacognitive processes (Pugh, 2020). These different models of therapy work with 'self-multiplicity' – referring not only to a person's different states of mind or modes, but also to working directly with those aspects. Chairwork is used in these types of therapy to separate the different sides, and to make them more concrete and accessible. For example, in CFT, additional chairs are used to represent the various sides of the client that have been aroused by an interpersonal conflict. In each of these chairs, the client interprets the different sides with a particular focus on their cognitive, physical, emotional and behavioural characteristics. Then, from the original therapy chair, the client makes contact with his or her 'compassionate self' and validates, empathises with and regulates the different sides.

1.3.7 Emotion-focused therapy

In the 1980s, Leslie Greenberg developed emotion-focused therapy (EFT) in collaboration with Sue Johnson. EFT can be seen as a synthesis of various humanistic therapies such as client-centred therapy, focusing, and Gestalt therapy (Kellogg, 2015). Chairwork is an essential element in EFT. Greenberg was also one of the first researchers to embark on scientific study of the effectiveness of chairwork and the functional mechanisms underlying it. An overview of research conducted to date on chairwork is given later in this chapter.

1.3.8 Schema therapy

Schema therapy has strong roots in cognitive behavioural therapy, but integrates cognitive and behavioural as well as emotion-focused interventions (Young et al., 2003). Since the first treatment study on the effectiveness of schema therapy in treating patients with borderline personality disorder (Giessen-Bloo et al., 2006), research on schema therapy and its applications has developed significantly. Although chairwork is only described briefly in the original book by Jeffrey Young et al., this technique is now one of the most widely used interventions within schema therapy (Van Genderen & Arntz, 2021; Arntz & Jacob, 2011; Hayes & Van der Wijngaart, 2018).

1.4 Forms of chairwork

As we have seen, chairwork is seen in various therapeutic frameworks as a powerful intervention that can make a meaningful contribution to the client's change process. So far, we have used the terms 'chairwork' and 'chair technique' broadly and interchangeably. Both these terms suggest that the technique always has the same form. However, there are in fact variants of this technique in practice, including an 'empty-chair technique' (in which one additional empty chair is used) and a 'multiple-chair technique' (in which the client sits on several chairs during the exercise). These different forms of chairwork are described briefly below.

1.4.1 The empty-chair technique

In this form of chairwork, an empty chair represents a person, a symptom or a particular side of the client. It might, for example, represent a significant attachment figure from the past who is at the root of present-day self-critical beliefs. In the exercise, a dialogue is conducted with the empty chair, which may also be placed at a physical distance – sometimes even outside the room.

1.4.2 The multiple-chair technique

In the multiple-chair technique the client inhabits, or plays the role of, their own different sides, and views their thoughts or feelings from two or more chairs. Dialogues between the different sides of the client then provide insights into the intrapersonal patterns. The multiple-chair technique can also be used to represent one or more other people, and therefore to investigate and work with interpersonal interactions. Here, the multiple-chair technique not only offers opportunities for diagnosis and insight but also provides an opportunity to try out new behaviours in the interactions that are played out between the client and those represented by the other chairs.

1.4.3 Types of dialogues

Another way to classify the different forms of chairwork is according to the types of dialogue they facilitate. *Internal* dialogue, or *intra*personal chairwork, involves talking to different sides of the person whereas *external* dialogue, or *inter*personal chairwork, is used to have dialogues between the client and people from their past, present or future. In his 'Four Dialogue Matrix', Scott

Kellogg (2018) links these internal and external dialogues to the use of one or more chairs. There are four different possible combinations in this matrix:

1. The use of a *single* chair for an *internal* dialogue with one side of the client.
2. The use of *multiple* chairs for an *internal* dialogue with multiple sides of the client.
3. The use of a *single* chair for an *external* dialogue with a traumatic event.
4. The use of *multiple* chairs for an *external* dialogue with several other people.

1.5 Scientific research on chairwork

Research on chairwork approaches is very diverse. The literature consists of two strands – research into the effects of chairwork on clients and their functioning, and research into the experiences of clients and therapists with the technique. Chairwork can be tested as a standalone treatment, or as part of a larger treatment. Studies into its effectiveness as part of a wider treatment have focused on a range of therapeutic and theoretical frameworks, but most commonly EFT and Gestalt therapy. EFT uses chairwork to promote self-compassion, and Gestalt therapy uses it to resolve internal and interpersonal conflicts. Below, we describe firstly the existing effectiveness studies, divided according to the therapeutic approach and the specific form of chairwork, and secondly those studies that have explored the experiences of clients and therapists. In both cases, we summarise key findings from research that could be relevant for clinical practice and readers of this book.

1.6 Research into the effectiveness of chairwork

1.6.1 Chairwork in schema therapy

Only one study has been published to date specifically on chairwork within schema therapy (Van Maarschalkerweerd et al., 2021). This study compared the effectiveness of an empty-chair intervention with a cognitive technique designed to reduce negative core beliefs in twenty clients with borderline personality disorder. All participants received both interventions in a single session. During the chairwork intervention, an empty chair was assigned to the client's punitive and critical inner voice, which was tackled by the therapist and eventually expelled from the treatment room. During the cognitive intervention, evidence for and against their punitive core cognition was identified, and the client was encouraged to formulate an alternative, more realistic conceptualisation.

Both techniques reduced the strength and credibility of the client's punitive core beliefs, and both increased the client's sense of control over their negative thoughts. Clients generally indicated that they experienced a significant emotional impact from the chairwork intervention, and that they expected it to be more effective for them than the cognitive technique if they were to move forward with additional therapy sessions. Further research is required to investigate whether the chair technique does indeed produce a stronger effect compared to this kind of cognitive intervention over multiple sessions, and, if so, how long the results last.

1.6.2 Chairwork in the 'court method' (cognitive therapy)

The 'court method' (Bögels & Van Oppen, 2019; Van der Wijngaart, 2015) is a cognitive therapy technique in which negative thoughts are challenged by collecting evidence for and against them from the different roles typically present in a courtroom (e.g. prosecutor, defence, jury). This technique can be performed in dialogue with the therapist or with chairs representing the different roles.

An observational study conducted with one-hundred-and-sixty-six clients in Brazil looked at the effect of the court method with and without the use of chairs (De Oliveira et al., 2012), and found it to be generally effective in reducing the credibility of negative beliefs. Whether or not chairs were used did not make a clear difference; however, the results may not be reliable as other factors may have influenced the results – for example clients were not randomised to conditions, and the interventions and measures were not standardized. A later study involving thirty-nine outpatient clients with a variety of symptoms compared chairwork in the court method to a court intervention in which the client played the different roles without moving between chairs (Delavechia et al., 2016). In this study, chairwork techniques appeared slightly more effective in reducing the credibility and emotional charge of the clients' negative beliefs.

These initial results do not provide clear support for or against the use of chairwork within the court method; research remains sparse, and the studies that exist have clear methodological limitations. Because of this, it is premature to draw conclusions on the effectiveness of chairwork in the court method; however, there do not seem to be any disadvantages to using chairs in this method, and clients indicate that they could see the potential of the technique over the course of several sessions.

1.6.3 The two-chair and the empty-chair in Gestalt therapy and EFT

Within Gestalt therapy and EFT there has been research into the effectiveness of the 'two-chair' and 'empty-chair' techniques. In the two-chair technique, clients usually identify two sides of themselves that enter into a dialogue with each other, with the ultimate goal of achieving reconciliation and greater integration. Research into the two-chair technique usually focuses on self-criticism and self-compassion (especially in EFT) or on internal conflicts such as making difficult decisions (especially in Gestalt therapy). Research into the empty-chair technique usually focuses on unresolved conflicts with others, especially in Gestalt therapy.

1.6.4 The two-chair technique with Generalised Anxiety Disorder (GAD)

In an exploratory study with eight clients, researchers developed a two-chair exercise specifically for generalised anxiety disorder (GAD) (Murphy et al., 2017). The exercise started by placing the client's 'anxious self' on a separate chair, with the initial aim of making the client aware of this aspect of their character. The function of this 'worrier' was then explored in conversation with it, and its emotional impact on the client was examined by going back to the original chair. The ultimate goal was to constrain the anxious self and allow the client's healthy side to set assertive boundaries around it. As expected, the researchers observed that clients experienced more general tension at the beginning of the exercise, showed more intense and specific emotions (such as anger and fear) in the middle of the exercise, and experienced relief and a sense of self-determination at the end. This study does not say anything directly about the effectiveness of this particular technique in relieving GAD symptoms, but it does give an idea of which processes (such as emotional processing and assigning meaning) could be addressed effectively by this form of chairwork.

1.6.5 The two-chair technique with self-critical clients

In a two-chair technique focused on self-criticism and self-compassion, clients who are highly self-critical are usually invited to place their 'internal critic' on a second chair. Seated in the first chair, the client receives the self-criticism and he or she responds to their internal critic by expressing their own emotions and needs. The client may move between the two chairs several times during the exercise. The goal is ultimately to integrate the two sides more, and to develop greater self-compassion (Neff et al., 2007; Sutherland et al., 2014).

A small-scale study with six participants experiencing major depressive symptoms, moderate anxiety symptoms and problems in emotion regulation investigated the feasibility and potential of an EFT group treatment using the two-chair technique and focusing on self-compassion as the central component (Robinson et al., 2014). The treatment consisted of nine weekly two-hour sessions. Psychoeducation was given in the first session, and attention was on closure in the last session. In the intervening seven sessions, the two-chair exercise was conducted for forty-five minutes each time with an individual client in front of the whole group. The treatment showed promise in reducing depression and anxiety. More pronounced effects were observed on emotion regulation. The results were sustained for one year after treatment; however, there was no control group, making it uncertain that the effects observed were specifically due to the treatment or the chair technique.

In a pilot study with nine highly self-critical participants, the two-chair exercise was spread over five to eight sessions (Shahar et al., 2012). Depression and anxiety symptoms as well as feelings of 'not being good enough' decreased immediately after treatment, and this result was sustained for up to six months. Further, the degree of self-hatred decreased during treatment, but this effect was not sustained. Six months after treatment, clients reported an increase in supportive thoughts. This pilot study indicates that the two-chair technique shows promise as a means to combat symptoms related to self-criticism. Once again, however, a limitation of this study was the lack of a control group, meaning we cannot be sure that the chair technique was the cause of the beneficial effects.

A similar, two-chair intervention was compared to a control group in another study (Stiegler et al., 2018a, 2018b). This study involved twenty-one clients with mild anxiety and mood symptoms. All participants at first received only supportive conversations that focused on the active therapeutic stance of emotion-focused therapy (expressing empathy, genuineness and unconditional positive appreciation). They then had five sessions with the two-chair technique. The phase involving chairwork showed a greater reduction in anxiety and depressive symptoms than the earlier phase. For self-criticism, it was striking that although the chairwork specifically focused on the client's self-critical side, the degree of self-criticism decreased similarly when chairwork was not used. At the individual level, the researchers saw that with the chair technique four subjects became more self-critical, eight became less so, and nine remained the same. In further analysis, the researchers explored the effect on emotional intensity and emotional processing, as seen in certain significant statements made by clients during the sessions. The chairwork approach seemed to be slightly more emotionally intense, although the degree of emotional processing seemed similar in both phases and the active mechanism of the chair technique in this form remains somewhat unclear.

Finally, the two-chair technique was used with a group of forty-five self-critical students with and without anger regulation problems (Kramer & Pascual-Leone, 2016; Nardone et al., 2021). The added value of a writing task aimed at expressing assertive needs and emotions was also tested in this study. Participants were first asked to recall a conflict or an experience of failure. They were then asked to sit on a chair representing their internal critic, to express their criticism of themselves in relation to this memory, and then to move to the receiver's chair to respond to the criticism. Next, they were given a writing task, in the first part of which they were asked what their needs were in the conflict or failure situation (e.g. appreciation, support) and invited to write about why they had these needs. In the second part of the writing task, they completed sentences representing an assertive response to their anger (for example: "I have the right to be confident because...") to prepare them for making an assertive response to their internal critic. After the writing task, the participants were again given the opportunity to respond to their internal critic from the receiving chair.

The participants indicated that the intervention had increased their sense of assertiveness. Indeed, observations showed that participants seemed to respond to their internal critic with less tension, fear or shame and with more assertiveness after the writing task than before, although participants with anger problems were less able to express their assertive needs to their internal critic. However, while participants were able to express their needs more effectively by examining them (for example through a writing task) in a session with a chair exercise, the strength of expression of emotions was not improved.

Furthermore, because this study did not include control groups without chairwork or without a writing task, the effects cannot simply be attributed to these respective interventions. Further research with appropriate control groups is needed to be more certain about these effects.

1.6.6 The two-chair technique focused on internal conflict

In Gestalt therapy research, the two-chair technique is generally used to explore and integrate conflicting feelings around a situation or problem, in which the chairs represent the conflicting feelings and thoughts. In a study with sixteen students, the two-chair approach was compared with empathic reflections by the therapist (Greenberg & Clarke, 1979). The study lasted two weeks, and participants were invited to bring something they were in doubt about (for example, whether or not to interact with someone who was a bad influence on them). In one week they had a session with the two-chair technique, and in the other their conflict was empathically reflected by the therapist.

In both sessions, participants felt equally understood by their therapist and found the therapist equally empathic. However, in the session with the chairwork, participants were more engaged in exploring and integrating the different sides of the conflict, and the chairwork led to a different understanding of their internal conflict twice as often as the empathic reflections alone. In a follow-up study, forty-two students were observed under one of three conditions: the two-chair technique, a focusing exercise with empathic reflections, or no intervention (Greenberg & Higgins, 1980). Compared to the control group, participants in both intervention groups were more aware of their internal conflict and were more solution-focused a week after the session. The two-chair technique also led to creating more new meaning than the focusing intervention.

Other research looked at the utility of the two-chair technique in arriving at a decision or solution to a problem. Forty-eight healthy participants received two sessions with the two-chair technique, two sessions with a solution-focused cognitive technique where the advantages and disadvantages of the various options were considered, or no intervention (Clarke & Greenberg, 1986). Compared to the control group, both interventions were found to be equally effective in reducing indecision one week after the last session. The effect was stronger with chairwork; however this did not translate into differences in the rate of actual decision making, which ultimately occurred equally in all three groups.

Another study that compared the two-chair approach with a cognitive decision-making technique was conducted with participants who were unsure about continuing a partner relationship (Trachsel et al., 2012). Participants received two sessions with either the two-chair technique or a cognitive intervention (listing the pros and cons of continuing or breaking the relationship) within two weeks, and a short telephone booster session one week later. The researchers also looked at processes that occurred during the sessions. The results showed that both interventions gave more clarity about the participants' decisions, and that the two-chair technique led to more insight into and integration of the different sides that played a role in the internal conflict around the relationship. There was a similar decrease in ambivalence around making a decision in both groups, and this was sustained for four months after the last session. Depressive symptoms decreased in the period from before the intervention to four months after the last session, but only in the cognitive intervention group.

The two-chair studies outlined above were all conducted on healthy participants, and their results might not generalise to clinical populations. However, one very small-scale study examined the effect of the two-chair approach on internal conflicts in three clients with psychological symptoms (Greenberg & Rice, 1981). Here, the two-chair technique was compared to an active empathic attitude from the therapist during ongoing treatment. The chair exercise led to more exploration of feelings and experiences, to personally meaningful integration of these experiences, or to intensely felt solutions to problems. Chairwork also seemed to give clients a greater sense that a meaningful change had taken place during the session. Overall, though, there has been little empirical research into the two-chair technique as a standalone intervention for clients with clinical problems.

1.6.7 The empty-chair technique focused on interpersonal conflict

The empty chair technique is used to process feelings around interpersonal conflicts by imagining that the other person with whom the client has an unresolved conflict is seated on an empty chair. It is used extensively in Gestalt therapy. The client is first invited to express his or her initial emotions towards the other person, then plays that other person (insofar as the client has experienced them) and expresses the primary emotions that they feel in relation to the conflict and the interpersonal needs that were not met. The goal is for the client to have a more nuanced experience of the other person, to understand them better or to hold them responsible for the hurt, and to come to terms with the conflict, find acceptance and see themselves as worthwhile.

One initial study compared the empty-chair technique with a psychoeducation group (Paivio & Greenberg, 1995). The participants were thirty-four adult volunteers who were experiencing negative feelings towards another person with whom they had had a conflict in the past. Half these cases involved conflict with a parent, but there were also conflicts with abusers, ex-partners, adult children or employers. The participants generally had mild mood and/or anxiety symptoms but were not in therapy. Half the participants received twelve sessions with the empty-chair technique. In the psychoeducation group, twelve sessions were devoted to theory about emotions in conflicts, but the participants did not share their own experiences and did not do any active exercises. Compared to the psychoeducation group, participants who had received the empty-chair intervention reported less psychological suffering, fewer hostile feelings towards the other person and a stronger feeling of being able to let go of the conflict. Follow ups at four months and one year with around half the participants showed that these improvements were sustained. Participants in the psychoeducation group did not have follow-up measurements, so it is not known what the gains were in this group.

Remarkably, specifically among participants who had worked with an abuser, feelings of hostility towards the other did not decrease with the empty-chair technique, and sometimes they even increased (hostility toward abusive figures within the psychoeducation group was unknown). A limitation of this study is that the chairwork was given individually, while the psychoeducation was given in a group setting. Therefore, it is possible that a lack of individual contact in the psychoeducation group, rather than the chairwork itself, contributed to the differences between the groups. Further, without another active intervention control, it is unknown whether changes were specific to chairwork; it is possible that any therapy in which personal experiences were shared might have been just as effective.

In a follow-up study, clients with mild symptoms of depression, anxiety and interpersonal problems received twelve to fourteen weekly sessions using the empty-chair technique (Greenberg & Malcolm, 2002). The researchers looked at video recordings of sessions to see what made the difference between clients who were successful in resolving the conflict and those who were not. In total, thirteen clients succeeded and nineteen did not. Clients who were successful expressed intense emotions more often than those who were unsuccessful. Further, all participants who succeeded in resolving the conflict had fully recovered, compared to 38% of the clients who were unable to do so. However, it was not possible to predict in advance which clients would succeed and which would not.

The impact of the empty-chair technique on emotional experience was investigated in a study with sixty-one students (Narkiss-Guez et al., 2015). The participants suffered from anger towards a significant person in their lives with whom they wanted to improve their relationship. They received an intervention in which the therapist first empathically reflected their anger, then focused on the pain of loss rather than blaming the significant other (a 'reframing' intervention). Following this, participants completed an empty-chair exercise in which they expressed their emotional experiences to the significant other on the empty chair. Here, the reframing phase and the chairwork were seen as two different, active interventions, and the earlier phases were labelled as preparatory phases. The sessions were recorded on video and reviewed together with the participant several days later. The participant was asked about his or her anger and sadness during each phase.

No clear difference between phases was found in terms of anger and sadness experienced. However, sadness was felt more strongly than anger during both the reframing and chairwork phases, with greater sadness experienced during the chair technique. The authors interpreted this as an indication that, during the active phases and especially during the empty-chair technique, a shift in meaning had taken place in which the initial anger had given way to underlying grief about the loss in the relationship. Because both techniques were offered to each participant in the same order, it is not possible to conclude that the differences found can be attributed to the specific techniques. The participants' evaluations of the emotions they experienced were also surveyed only a few days after the session, which may have distorted their assessment and made it less reliable.

1.6.8 Multiple chair techniques within a broader treatment

The studies discussed above investigated specific chair techniques, either as standalone interventions or within a multi-component treatment. However, treatments can include several forms of chairwork. One thirty-two person study compared person-centred counselling (a basic empathic attitude) with and without additional experiential techniques, including the two-chair technique (focused on self-critical speech), the empty-chair technique (focused on interpersonal conflicts) and body-centred focusing (Goldman et al., 2006).

The clients had a diagnosis of a depressive disorder and received nine to twenty individual treatment sessions. Both forms of treatment had a beneficial effect on depressive symptoms and general psychological suffering (but not on self-esteem or interpersonal problems), and the treatment with the additional experiential techniques had the greatest effect. However, because the condition containing experiential techniques included two different techniques (focusing as well as chairwork), firm conclusions cannot be drawn as to what benefits, if any, were specifically due to the use of chairwork.

1.6.9 Summary and conclusions: the effectiveness of chairwork

Research on the effects of chairwork is diverse, in terms of both the form of chairwork investigated and the outcome measures used. This makes the literature rich, but also difficult to integrate. It is notable that research into chairwork in the context of schema therapy is sparse; we found only one published study (Van Maarschalkerweerd et al., 2021). However, the various studies do produce an overall picture in which chair techniques appear to be promising in reducing the credibility of negative thoughts, and are also experienced at a more emotional level in this regard than verbal cognitive techniques. This corresponds to the experiential and physical nature of chairwork.

More generally, the use of chairwork seems to enable clients to achieve a different perspective on their symptoms or the problems they face, and to gain more insight into them. This may also lead to them feeling more in control of their internal processes, which are represented by the various chairs. Finally, there seems to be evidence that chairwork can reduce psychological symptoms such as anxiety and mood problems. However, most of the studies had significant methodological limitations (e.g. small sample size, lack of a control group, limited sessions, no long-term follow-up), and more and better controlled researched is therefore needed to obtain certainty about these findings.

1.7 Research into the experiences of clients and therapists with chairwork

1.7.1 Clients' experiences with chair techniques

In two of the studies described above, clients were interviewed about their experiences after the event. In the EFT group approach study with self-critical clients by Robinson and colleagues (2014), those interviewed found chairwork to be the most powerful part of the treatment. They especially appreciated its 'here-and-now' quality, and they felt that it led to new insights and a change they could 'feel'. Participants also noted that they did not find the exercise easy; they anticipated it with tension and experienced it as intense and challenging. Similar feedback was reported from the two-chair intervention in individual EFT treatments (Stiegler et al., 2018). Here, again, clients initially found the idea of a chair exercise uncomfortable or embarrassing. Yet these clients too mostly found the two-chair exercise to be emotional yet also very meaningful, indicating that they gained more insight into their own influence and part in the self-critical dialogue that had become so familiar to them.

In a different study, twelve participants with a depressive disorder who were undergoing CFT treatment were asked about their perceptions of a chair technique intervention that focused on a dialogue between their critical side, their criticised side, and a compassionate side (Bell et al., 2019). The researchers looked first at the emotional and physical experience of the participants. The physical nature of the chairwork seemed to be very important to them. For example, they seemed to adopt a different body posture when changing chairs (e.g. more slouched on the criticised chair). Such physical differences helped them to understand the different sides of themselves better, and to distinguish them from each other. The physical distance between the different chairs, and therefore the demarcation between the different sides of the person, also gave a sense of psychological space that allowed clients to look at themselves more easily from a different perspective. Finally, the participants reported strong and varied emotions during the exercise, which seems appropriate for the awareness of different sides and perspectives and the experiential nature of the chair technique.

The researchers then analysed the cognitive experience of the same group of clients (Bell et al., 2020), and found that the insight that the clients had several sides to themselves helped them to arrive at new perspectives. Because the struggle between their different sides became visible in the chairs, they also gained insight into its intensity. Additionally, participants reported that, during the chair exercise, they spontaneously formed mental images of their different sides (older/younger, smaller/bigger, with or without certain emotions, etc.) which they placed on the different chairs in their imagination. This also helped in distinguishing the different sides. Such images were often related to specific, unpleasant, often early memories (for example, being bullied at school).

Nine clients with a depressive disorder who were undergoing CFT treatment were asked about their experiences with the multiple chair exercise (Bell et al., 2021), and several themes emerged. Firstly, the differentiation of the various emotions using chairwork led to an appreciation of the emotional complexity of clients' experiences of interpersonal conflict. This helped to distinguish emotions and reduced the more generalised and diffuse bad feelings that they had had previously. Clients were able to recognise that some emotions, such as fear and anger, were often dominant, but they also discovered new emotions around the conflict, such as sadness, that had not been experienced as clearly before. Another theme was the procedure of the technique itself. Clients found that chairwork led to greater felt emotions and emotional intensity than talking about their emotions in a more rational way. The emotions were more present, as it were. Physically moving between chairs also helped clients to distance themselves from emotions left behind in a chair, and to consciously take a different perspective when changing chairs. This enabled them to identify with their emotions less strongly, and to look at them with more distance.
In this form of chairwork, one chair is reserved for the 'compassionate self'. Clients noticed that they could indeed be more compassionate, and integrate their various emotional sides better, from this chair. This compassionate side felt somewhat like a parent, looking after and taking care of the various more childish emotional sides.

In a study specifically on eating disorders, nine participants with a diagnosis of anorexia nervosa were asked about their experiences with a chair intervention focused on the 'voice' of the eating disorder (Ling et al., 2021). In this kind of voice dialogue, the voice (or side) of the eating disorder is placed on a separate chair (or the same chair in another place in the room). The eating disorder voice is then invited to express itself – what it looks like, what its intentions are, where it comes from, what thoughts it represents and so on. Participants indicated that this technique allowed them to feel more distance from the eating disorder voice, and to gain more space for other perspectives. They also reported a greater understanding of the function of the eating disorder voice, as well as its disadvantages, and said that the technique gave them increased hope for recovery.

One study explored willingness to engage in a chair exercise (Muntigl et al., 2020). The participants were clients with a diagnosis of depression, who were receiving EFT treatment. Of the twenty-six proposals to do a chair exercise that the researchers examined, in five cases the client agreed immediately. In fifteen cases there was clear hesitation on the part of the client (for example silence in response), and in six cases the client refused immediately. The client was more likely to agree immediately if the therapist formulated the proposal tactfully (for example, "would you like to try that?") and clearly left the choice to the client. Hesitation or rejection were more likely if it was unclear to the client how the exercise would fit with their concerns or needs at that time. Further explanation by the therapist of the rationale and procedure of the exercise was sometimes effective in convincing the client, provided that the therapist showed flexibility and clearly tried to take a collaborative approach. The therapist's connection to and sensitivity for not only verbal but also non-verbal hesitation on the part of the client was very important.

1.7.2 Therapists' experiences with chair techniques

A survey of British cognitive behavioural therapists interested in chairwork showed that the vast majority found it appropriate within the framework of CBT, and rated its value and effectiveness highly. However, few had received any formal training in chairwork and most therefore doubted their knowledge and ability (Pugh et al., 2021). Those who had received training felt more skilled – and the more skilled they felt, the more often they used the technique. Participants also indicated that they found chairwork particularly useful in helping clients to access emotions and experience multiple perspectives. While some therapists were deterred by the great emotional impact of chairwork as they had concerns about distressing their clients, this fear predominantly affected those who had not been trained in chairwork and was not an issue for more experienced therapists.

The COVID-19 pandemic saw many therapists and clients moving to online therapy and, as part of this, experience was gained with chairwork online. A survey of forty-one therapists produced a picture of this experience (Pugh et al., 2021). Most acknowledged that they were initially somewhat sceptical about using chairwork online; however, about two-thirds ultimately felt that chairwork went as well and as smoothly online as it did in the therapy room. One third found it to be less effective, noting that sessions remained more superficial and were more likely to involve "talking about" emotions rather than activating emotional experiences. The advantages and disadvantages of having clients receive the therapy in their home settings were also mentioned. For example, some therapists thought that clients might find it more difficult to immerse themselves in the exercise because they had to function in the home environment immediately afterwards. There were also concerns about privacy at times. The advantages included, for instance, that the home environment could be a safe place and that insights learned could be applied more quickly in everyday life.

Therapists were sometimes frustrated that they were not physically present when a client did a chair exercise, because they felt less able to support them. Other clients seemed to benefit from this distance and to take on more ownership of the exercise, which contributed to the development of their autonomy. Of course, technical and practical obstacles were also mentioned such as disruptions, restricted space and field of vision, missing non-verbal cues, and limited resources. The therapists and clients often shared responsibility for these obstacles, which led to finding creative solutions together. These experiences produced various tips such as using headphones, making sure there was good lighting, and having a 'plan B' in case of problems with Internet connections. It was also found to be useful to provide longer, more thorough verbal explanation in preparation for chairwork, and to direct the steps more closely during the exercise than would be usual in the therapy room.

The use of chairs took place in different ways. For example, clients could arrange the same setup at home as in the therapy room, move around the room on the same chair, or use other objects or places that could be linked to their different sides. Finally, extra attention was paid in online sessions to 'warming up' and 'cooling down' (for example, in the form of an imagery exercise), so the client had time to transition back into the home situation. How the effectiveness of chairwork online compares to chairwork in the therapy room has not yet been investigated. Based on this survey, effectiveness seems to depend at least in part on the extent to which there is specific attention paid to possible obstacles in preparation, on creativity, and on clear guidance from the therapist.

1.7.3 Summary and conclusions: the experiences of clients and therapists

Regarding clients' experiences with chairwork, three points stand out. Firstly, there is a distinct cognitive experience; clients indicate that chairwork facilitates them taking different perspectives and gaining more insight into their symptoms or problems. Secondly, there is a clear 'felt' experience: physically moving between chairs combined with the here-and-now nature of chairwork means that any insights are felt and not just rationally understood. Clients report a rich emotional experience in which imagination also seems to play a role (for example, in spontaneously forming images of the characters in the chairs). Thirdly, chairwork can be challenging for clients – the approach may seem strange or uncomfortable at first, and this is experienced as a barrier. The exercise itself is usually experienced as very intense and powerful, but clients may also feel resistance. Finally, clients seem more willing to do a chair exercise if the benefits and procedure are made clear to them, and if they feel that they are free to decide, in consultation with the therapist, whether or not to proceed with it.

Regarding the attitudes of therapists towards chairwork techniques, it is notable that the enhancement of emotional experience is mentioned as a valuable element. When therapists are less trained in chairwork, they tend to be more fearful of the emotional impact of the technique; however, this is not a concern for experienced therapists. Although understandable and human, this anxiety does not seem justified in view of the available literature, and we hope that this book will contribute to an increased confidence in handling and using chair techniques. Therapists also seem to be able to adapt chairwork to an online format effectively. Good preparation, more explicit and direct guidance, and flexibility and creativity on both sides are recommended in order to make this a success and to take the advantages of the online format over the therapy room environment. The use of the chairwork online is discussed more concretely in Chapter 8 in this book.

1.8 Chairwork in schema therapy – the basis of this book

As we have seen, chairwork is used in various therapeutic movements and comes in various forms. However, in this book we have chosen to limit our exploration of chairwork to one single therapeutic framework – schema therapy. Besides motives of readability and clarity, there were two key reasons for this. Firstly, chairwork is commonly used as an intervention in schema therapy and, due to the enormous growth in the popularity and application of schema therapy, this therapeutic model is already familiar, at least to some extent, to many therapists around the world. And secondly, the author himself has a great deal of experience with chairwork in a schema therapy context.

Although we will focus throughout on schema therapy, it should be noted that the descriptions and examples of chairwork in this book are by no means limited to this therapeutic modality. Indeed, the content can be translated quite readily to other therapeutic frameworks; the concepts and language may differ, but the principles and steps are largely the same. For those readers who are less familiar with schema therapy, a brief introduction to the model and its key concepts is given below.

1.8.1 Schema therapy

Schema therapy is an integrative form of psychotherapy that was developed in the 1990s by Jeffrey Young (Young et al., 2003). Schema therapy is characterised by three defining aspects:

- The language/concepts of basic needs, schemas and modes.
- A therapeutic relationship based on limited reparenting.
- The integration of cognitive, behavioural and emotion-oriented techniques (in particular, imagery rescripting and chairwork).

1.8.2 The language and concepts of schemas and modes

Schema therapy is centred on the presence of basic emotional needs (Arntz et al., 2021) that are assumed to apply to all human beings, as if they are part of our DNA. When these basic emotional needs are adequately validated, emotional development leading to an emotionally healthy adult occurs. However, when there are chronic deficits in the fulfilment of these basic emotional needs – depending also on the individual's temperament and other psychological and social factors – dysfunctional schemas may arise, such as the Emotional Deprivation schema or the Mistrust schema.

These schemas can be seen as emotional 'wounds' – a clustering of emotional, cognitive and physiological responses that are coloured by a certain theme, such as the perception that one's own feelings are not important or that other people cannot be trusted. Though they were created in early childhood, current circumstances in the client's adult life can activate these schemas, triggering overly strong emotional and behavioural reactions. The state of mind that a person then experiences is called a 'mode' – an aspect or side of the client that determines the way they think, feel and act in that moment. In other circumstances, other modes can be activated, meaning that the client will switch modes throughout the day. Four categories of modes are distinguished:

- Child modes
- Coping modes
- Parent modes
- The Healthy Adult mode

Child modes

Child modes relate to the emotional sides of the client – the states of mind in which natural emotional responses are experienced. These emotional responses are coloured by the deficits that the client has experienced in their past, which make the emotions more violent or intense than the trigger in the present would justify or explain. The aim of the therapy is to validate the deficit in needs that lies at the root of the client's emotional pain.

Coping modes

Coping modes can be seen as the sides of the client that enable them to survive. The primary coping mode, also called the Protector, has a defensive function with the aim of minimising underlying vulnerability, fear, sadness or anger that is the result of activated schemas. The overwhelming emotional experiences of the child modes can be kept at bay through avoidance, surrender or reversal. In a sense, we all have a 'Protector' – a side that helps us to feel safer in situations where vulnerability or emotions could be dangerous or non-functional – and this can be a useful and adaptive response. The problem with a client's Protector is typically not the mode itself, but the fact that clients do not have any control over it. The aim of therapy is to reduce the dominance of these Protectors, in order to enable more contact with the underlying emotions and needs.

Parent modes

Parent modes are the states of mind in which clients judge themselves in ways that they have experienced being judged in the past by important attachment figures. The characterisation 'parent' refers to the fact that parents are often the most important attachment figures and thus the source of these internalised self-assessments, but they can equally be other significant figures such as grandparents, other relatives, teachers or childhood peers. We all carry internalised messages from the past; however, clients' messages are often punishing (the 'punitive parent' mode), perfectionist (the 'demanding parent' mode) or represent an inner critic (the 'guilt-inducing parent' mode). It is these internalised messages that have contributed to the symptom patterns. Schema therapy aims to reduce these messages and replace them with healthier, often more nuanced, self-assessments.

The Healthy Adult mode

The Healthy Adult can be seen as the 'captain of the ship' or 'manager of the team', where the crew or team members are the other modes. In the Healthy Adult mode, an individual is able to recognise activated self-criticism, evoked emotions and reflexive survival strategies, and handle them in a healthy way – maintaining contact with their basic needs and other people. It should be noted that being a healthy adult does not mean experiencing balance, reason and happiness all the time. The aim of schema therapy is to strengthen the healthy side of the client, not to erase all other modes.

1.8.3 A therapeutic relationship based on limited reparenting

Chronic symptoms and personality problems arise when clients grow up in environments with many negative, sometimes traumatic, learning experiences. The client's self-image and their image of others is formed by these internalised experiences. The consequence is that the individual's emotional development stagnates, and the growing child learns only to survive under difficult conditions. The aim of schema therapy is to help the client to internalise more healthy messages and experiences, so that their stagnated emotional development can be reactivated. This is a complex process, and a simple cognitive insight or change in behaviour is often insufficient to achieve it.

Limited reparenting involves establishing a professional therapeutic attachment relationship in which, within the limits of professional conduct, the therapist acts as a role model of the healthy parent that the client should have had in the past. Healthy experiences are gained within this new attachment relationship, which can counterbalance previously internalised negative experiences. This therapeutic relationship is characterised by the therapist's own individual approach, with those basic needs that are lacking being met in a more personal way. For example, the therapist might make him or herself more accessible to the client in times of need, or step into the picture during an imagery exercise to fight antagonists and provide emotional care for the 'child'.

1.8.4 The integration of cognitive, behavioural and emotion-focused techniques

There are many methods and techniques that can be used to achieve the goal of fulfilling a client's basic needs in a personal way. Schema therapy integrates a range of cognitive, behavioural and experiential techniques that are also commonly used in other therapeutic frameworks. In particular, the use of experiential (or emotion-focused) techniques bridges the gap between 'knowing' and 'feeling' for many clients. The experiential techniques that are most commonly-used in schema therapy are imagery rescripting, historical roleplay and chairwork. In imagery rescripting, meaningful images are visualised and corrective emotional experiences are gained by changing those images or the course of the visualised events. In historical roleplay, significant events from the client's past are re-enacted to provide more insight into the origins of their present emotional deficits, and to give them the opportunity to advocate for not having had their basic needs met in the historical scenario.

1.8.5 Chairwork in schema therapy

Chairwork is one of the most commonly-used experiential techniques in schema therapy. As we have seen, chairwork involves the use of chairs to represent different modes. The client is asked to sit in a specific chair, project themselves into a specific mode and talk about experiences from this specific state of mind; they then move to another chair. By having the client project themself into a different mode on the second chair and asking them to respond to the same experiences as were considered in the first chair, a dialogue between the client's different sides can be stimulated.

1.8.6 Chairwork in the phases of schema therapy treatment

In schema therapy, chairwork can be used in each phase of treatment (analysis, initial, middle and final phase). However, the exact method will change through the phases. An overview of chair techniques typically used in the various phases of treatment is given below.

Phase of treatment	Application
Case conceptualisation	Chairs for diagnostics; exploring modes
Initial phase	Chairs to identify modes Negotiating with Protector Fighting parent modes Validating the needs of Child modes
Middle phase	Coaching the Healthy Adult (HA) Practicing the three steps to the HA
Final phase	Strengthening the HA

1.8.7 Practical requirements for working with chairs

Chairwork requires some space in the therapy room to position the different chairs. The traditional table between the therapist's chair and the client's chair is something of an obstacle when taking different positions during chair exercises, and it is therefore preferable to arrange chairs for the therapist and the client without this table barrier in between.

Working with chairs is also difficult when the chairs are bulky and heavy and therefore harder to move. If possible, provide several lightweight folding chairs that can be taken out when needed for chairwork. When working with a client's different sides or modes, it is helpful if the chairs have distinctive features – for example different colours or shapes. These differences can help the client (and the therapist!) to keep everything clear and organized in a multiple chair technique.

1.9 Chapter Summary

Chairwork is a set of procedures in which chairs are used to represent experiences, symptoms, thoughts, sides of the client or significant others. Working with these representations makes it possible to initiate dialogues between the different sides. These exercises can lead to insights into intrapersonal or interpersonal dynamics, and ultimately to corrective emotional experiences.

We have given a brief outline of the development of chairwork within different theoretical and therapeutic frameworks over time, and we have explained that a schema therapy perspective was chosen for this book. To help non-schema therapists follow the text, a short overview of the key characteristics of schema therapy has been provided. In the rest of the book, the concepts and language from schema therapy will be used, but the strategies, examples and variants of the technique can also be applied in other therapeutic frameworks with just a few minor adjustments.

An overview of research undertaken to date on chairwork has also been given. Only limited research has been done, and most studies had significant methodological limitations, but chairwork does appears to be potentially effective in reducing the credibility of negative thoughts – and it is also experienced at a more emotional level in this regard than verbal cognitive techniques. The insights that clients gain are typically 'felt' through the exercise, and not just rationally understood. More generally, the use of chairwork appears to make it possible for clients to experience a different perspective on their symptoms or problems and to gain more insight into them. There is also evidence that chairwork can reduce psychological symptoms such as anxiety and mood problems. Chairwork is experienced as intense and powerful, but it is also often strange and uncomfortable at first. Explaining the purpose and the procedure helps with client willingness. Therapists consider the emotional experience in the exercise to be valuable; education and experience has been found to calm initial fears, and to contribute to therapist confidence in handling and using the technique.

1.10 Case studies in this book

For the sake of continuity, we will use two running case studies throughout this book – Nicky and Greg. These are fictitious clients, but their stories, symptoms and examples are based on real individuals. Nicky and Greg were also used as case studies in the book Imagery Rescripting: Theory and Practice (Van der Wijngaart, 2021), and the audio-visual production 'Fine Tuning Chairwork' (Hayes & Van der Wijngaart, 2018).

Nicky

Nicky is a twenty-eight-year-old woman with borderline personality disorder, dependent personality disorder and recurrent depressive episodes. She tends to avoid situations of potential conflict with others, but as a result of built-up tensions she can sometimes have outbursts of anger. These symptoms have been going on for years, and are related to a childhood in which she lacked security due to violence and emotional neglect on one hand, and a lack of self-expression and autonomy due to overprotection on the other. She grew up as an only child in a family with an aggressive father who regularly verbally abused her, but who was sometimes also overprotective. Her mother drank regularly and was emotionally absent. Nicky's grandmother was the only safe attachment figure available to her, but she saw her only sporadically and she died when Nicky was twenty-three.

Nicky's self-image is very negative: she thinks of herself as stupid, complaining and hopeless. She distrusts other people, often feels that others don't like her, and is afraid of being abandoned. As in childhood, she still often feels anxious, lonely and sad. She tries to negate this pain by disconnecting from her feelings or conforming to what others want out of fear of being abandoned.

Greg

Greg is a forty-one-year-old man with persistent depressive disorder and an alcohol dependency in long-term partial remission. He comes from a family with a cold, distant father, who was not aggressive but was demanding and indirectly gave Greg the message that he was not interested in him. His mother, although emotionally softer, was not able to compensate for his father's dominant, demanding upbringing. As a child Greg felt, saw and heard how unhappy his mother was in her marriage with his father. For instance, his mother would complain to him about his father, was openly sad and depressed in Greg's presence, and would say things like, "No one cares how I feel."

Greg has always felt that he was inadequate and should do better. He looks at the world around him in the manner his father taught: "In the end, you're on your own in life. Don't complain, just take it." He has internalised his mother's messages into a self-image that is coloured by a sense of not being strong enough and not supportive enough for others. His survival strategy has been to turn this feeling of inadequacy into a dominant, sometimes devaluing attitude.

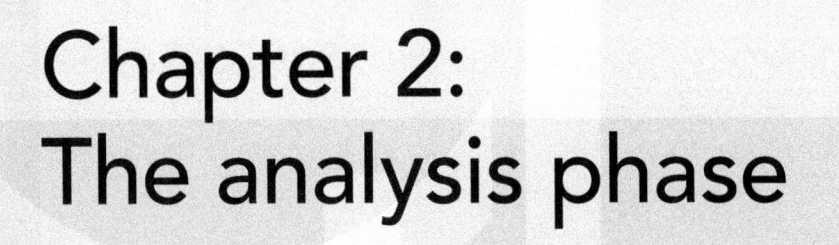

Chapter 2:
The analysis phase

Chapter 2: The analysis phase

Chapter map	
2.1	Introduction
2.2	Chairwork in the analysis phase
2.3	Chapter summary

2.1 Introduction

This chapter will explore how chairwork can be used to gain more insight into the different modes in which clients might find themselves, and the dynamics that may exist between those modes.

Clients usually come to therapy with symptoms and problems that they do not fully understand. They may feel sad, anxious, angry or guilty, but it is often unclear to them exactly what is going on in situations when these feelings are activated. The first step in any therapy is therefore the analysis phase, when both therapist and client gain an understanding of the symptoms and problems. In schema therapy, the aim of the analysis phase is to become aware of the client's relevant modes and the dynamics between them. Awareness requires a certain mental and emotional distance from one's own experience – a transition from identifying with an experience to becoming aware of it, making it possible to look at and reflect on that experience. Chairwork is ideal for creating such awareness. In the multiple chair technique, the client speaks from various modes while sitting in different chairs. This causes those chairs to become physical representations of their assigned modes, which can then be examined and discussed with the therapist. Using chairwork in the analysis phase also gives the client a clear message that the use of experiential exercises will be an integrated part of the therapy.

2.2 Chairwork in the analysis phase

There is no strict protocol for chairwork, and there are many ways to implement it. However, if you are concerned about your inexperience with the technique, the following step-by-step plan can be used as a guide. Each step of this plan is discussed in detail and explained with examples below.

Step-by-step plan for chairwork in the analysis phase	
Step 1: Choose the technique	
Step 2: Name the mode	
Step 3: Rationale for the technique	
Step 4: Have the client sit on another chair	
Step 5: Interview the mode	
Step 6: Add an extra chair or chairs for any other modes	
Step 7: Back to the original chair and reflection	
Step 8: Homework	

2.2.1 Step 1: Choose the technique

In the analysis phase, a variety of methods may be used to understand the client's symptoms and their relationship to meaningful learning experiences from their past. Typically questionnaires are given, childhood photos are reviewed, and a diagnostic visualisation exercise and chairwork are undertaken. When to use chairwork in the analysis phase is determined by several factors. It can be helpful to consider it as a standard part of the analysis phase, and to put it on the agenda in advance for a specific session. Table 2.1 gives an example of how the analysis phase could be structured, showing the place allocated to chairwork among other components.

Table 2.1: Overview of the analysis phase

Session	Method/technique
1	Exploration of symptoms, current situation, background, previous treatments and request for help now, downward arrow technique.
	Decision to use schema therapy and continuation of case conceptualisation. Sending questionnaires SCID-5-S and SCID-5-P (Structured Clinical Interview for DSM-5).
2	Administer SCID-5-S; client is asked to bring photos from their childhood for the next session.
3	View childhood photos and diagnostic imagery.
4	Give SCID-5-P.
	Send YSQ (Young Schema Questionnaire) and SMI (Schema Mode Inventory) by email.
5	Discuss YSQ and SMI results and link those outcomes to background and current symptom patterns.
6	Chairwork is used for diagnostics and a provisional mode model is drawn up.
	Multidisciplinary intake meeting with discussion of proposed treatment.
7	Go through report and (descriptive) diagnosis. Give report to client.
8	Discuss any questions and changes. Submit treatment plan and advise client to purchase the self-help book *Breaking Negative Thinking Patterns*.

Introducing chairwork – Nicky

>>Therapist: "Today, I want to do an exercise that I think will help us understand better why you sometimes get so stuck. It's a bit different to how we've been working so far, but in my experience this technique has the potential to help us move forward. We'll use chairs, and we'll assign the different states of mind that you experience in relation to your symptoms to specific chairs."

Chairwork works well when a client is stuck in a specific mode. For example, one client might present as full of shame and talk about believing they are bad, another might be fearful, talking about the certainty that bad things will happen, and another may emotionlessly say that they feel nothing at all. When a client is stuck in a specific mode, they appear completely immersed in that perspective and convinced that their thoughts are facts, as if there is no possible alternative point of view. By having the client sit on a different chair and speak from the presenting perspective, the new chair is 'charged' with that perspective and comes to represent it. The chair may then cue feelings associated with that side of the client – when the client sits in that chair, he or she feels those emotions (e.g. anxious, guilty, or indeed nothing at all). Furthermore, by then asking the client to get up from that chair and sit in another chair, the client not only experiences physical distance from the chair itself, but also emotional distance from the emotions with which it is now 'charged'. This emotional distance offers room for them to achieve more insight into that side of themselves.

There may also be reasons to introduce chairwork to address specific issues. A client may be embroiled in an internal conflict, for instance – where healthy intentions to participate in activities are inhibited by anxious avoidance, or a need for self-expression triggers guilt. By having two chairs represent these two different perspectives, this inward conflict can be made visible.

Finally, chairwork can be used to make visible modes that have not yet been explicitly identified but which the therapist expects to be present. For example, a dependent client may speak mainly about fear of losing others and their consequent tendency to conform to others' opinions. Conversely, they may not mention other feelings – for instance the anger, frustration or irritation that they must inevitably experience whenever their own needs are pushed aside. We might expect that a dependent client's learning history would have taught them to suppress their anger to a point where they no longer seem able to contact it. The therapist can assign a chair in order to make that restrained or avoided anger more visible to the client, and to explore it further. This is important because anger can be a natural source of strength, and strength is required to break what are often deep-set patterns. Expressing anger, alongside sadness or joy, is also a natural and necessary step in the process of learning to regulate emotions.

Recognising modes – Nicky

>>Nicky: "And so I just went along with them, even though I didn't really feel like it..."

>>Therapist: "And how did that make you feel? That you weren't really doing what you wanted to, and that they were getting their way?"

> **>>Nicky:** "It's okay... it's not that bad or anything... and it was actually fun in the end."
>
> **>>Therapist:** "I think it's great that you can talk like this about moments that are difficult for you. And I understand what you mean – the concern that others might be disappointed, the resulting fear you feel, and your tendency just to accommodate others. I wonder what happened to the frustration or annoyance you had though, that you couldn't do what you wanted. Where did that go?"
>
> **>>Nicky:** "Well, I wasn't angry though."
>
> **>>Therapist:** "No, I hear that you don't see it that way. But anger is just a normal human emotion, not something we choose; it's in our DNA. All babies cry when they're hungry, and that crying can start out soft and sad. But if you wait too long, sooner or later the baby will scream furiously. Some might do this faster than others; that's a matter of temperament. But every baby will do it at some point; sadness and anger are two sides of the same coin. How does that sound to you?"
>
> **>>Nicky:** "Yes, that makes sense in itself, but I don't feel angry or anything."
>
> **>>Therapist:** "Exactly! That's still missing from your story. I don't want to push anything onto you, but it seems like it would be a very normal reaction to be frustrated when you don't get what you want or need. And it also seems that you're finding it difficult to connect with that anger. That's why I'd like to add this chair now *[therapist takes an extra chair and puts it near the client]*. Let's make this the chair for anger, or annoyance. Or if that's too strong, the chair of 'not really liking that...' Could you sit in the chair for a moment and try to connect with that feeling of 'not liking that...'?"

2.2.2 Step 2: Name the mode

Whether the client is stuck in an emotional experience, has an inner conflict, or is experiencing a lack of specific feelings, chairwork starts by explicitly defining and naming the mode that the client is in as a distinct aspect of them. A simple way to introduce modes is to highlight their contrasts – the differences in the client's point of view: "I hear different perspectives, and perhaps they aren't just different perspectives but actually different sides of yourself." Identifying and defining the different sides, aspects or states of mind of the client and associating them with chairs comes first; the client physically moving to those chairs follows in Step 4. If the client has an inner conflict, then the contrast between the different perspectives in that inner conflict will be easy to identify.

> ### Confirming modes – Nicky
>
> *The therapist has heard Nicky say that she struggles between wanting to stay home and at the same time being afraid that others won't like her if she doesn't go out with them. Now the therapist wants to translate that internal struggle into modes.*
>
> **>>Therapist:** "So, I hear two different sides to your experience. On the one hand you didn't really want to go out with them, and you had other things you needed to do that day. But on the other hand, you were worried that you'd disappoint them if you stayed home. These are really two different perspectives, perhaps two different sides of you – one part of you that has its own needs and another 'Pleaser' part that conforms to others for fear of disappointing them. Does that sound right?"

However, when the client is stuck in a particular perspective, a contrast may not be immediately perceptible to them – in which case, as a therapist, you will have to explore other perspectives yourself – those you can discern or, for example, those you can gather based on the client's file.

> ### Recognising modes – Greg
>
> **>>Greg:** "I don't feel much, just neutral, nothing special."
>
> **>>Therapist:** "And have there been moments in the past week when you felt more cheerful, or a bit worse?"
>
> **>>Greg:** "No, just what I said, I don't feel that much at all."
>
> **>>Therapist:** "Maybe something else has been going on that kept you busy?"
>
> **>>Greg:** "No… well yes. I did have a fight with a friend, and she did go crazy, screaming and everything, but it didn't bother me that much."
>
> **>>Therapist:** "Okay, so you don't feel anything now, and actually you haven't felt much all week. Of course, it's quite normal to feel more sometimes and less at other times. But it does sound unusual that all feeling seems to be gone – even when you had a fight – and this has lasted all week. And it's not as if you're just not a very emotional person. I've got to know you as an emotional person, and in fact it's something I like about you. For instance, I clearly remember that we talked last time about how sad you felt that things weren't going the way you wanted them to. But it's completely different now, and all your feelings seem to be gone. It seems there are different sides to your experience – sometimes you can feel sad, but at other times, like now, you don't feel anything at all. You're flat and neutral, even though you're bringing up very emotional things that have happened, like the argument with your friend. Do I have that about right?"
>
> **>>Greg:** "Yes, exactly…"

Identifying and defining the different perspectives is the first step in the chair technique. These contrasts in experience can then be explored further on different chairs. It is helpful to support the identification of these experiences with gestures. Gesturing to a certain spot in the therapy room when a particular aspect of the client or their experience is referred to will place that perspective more externally to the client and give it more form. With this done, the transition to assigning a chair and physically placing the client in it becomes a logical next step.

> **Using gestures to reinforce physical space association – Nicky**
>
> **>>Therapist:** "So I hear two different sides to your experience. On the one hand *[therapist points to a spot to Nicky's right]*, you didn't really want to go with them, and you had other things you needed to do that day. But on the other hand *[therapist now points to a spot to Nicky's left]*, you were also so concerned about disappointing them that you went with them anyway. These two experiences are perhaps two different sides of you – one side that has its own needs *[therapist again points to the spot to Nicky's right]* and another 'Pleaser' side that conforms to others out of a fear of disappointing them *[therapist again gestures to the spot to Nicky's left]*.

What if…

…when describing their experience, the client keeps saying "That's really how it is!"?

Identifying and defining the experience is meant as a transition from simply describing the client's experience to a form of metacommunication, talking about that experience. Some clients feel so tied to the experience itself that it is difficult for them to make that transition. They perceive defining the experience as questioning it, which tends to make them try to convince you that what they are saying is correct. Don't get into a discussion about that; just repeat your observation that there are different experiences, and whether or not they are accurate they all differ from each other.

> ### Challenging perceptions – Nicky
>
> *[The therapist has just heard two different experiences from Nicky – a need to do something differently to how others suggest, but also the belief that she needs to conform because others will be disappointed in her if she doesn't join in.]*
>
> **>>Nicky:** "Yes, but it really is true, they've said the same thing about another friend – they thought she was just boring because she never went along!"
>
> **>>Therapist:** "Exactly! Now I'm hearing again that belief that you'd better accommodate them out of the fear that they might be disappointed in you if you don't."
>
> **>>Nicky:** "It's not a fear, that's really how it is."
>
> **>>Therapist:** "Yes, I know that's how it seems for you; once you're into that feeling *[pointing to the spot to Nicky's left]*, it's not a 'fear', it's a certainty. So it sounds wrong when I talk about 'sides' and 'fear' because for you, when you're in that experience *[points again]*, it's just reality. Is that true?"
>
> **>>Nicky:** "Yes…"
>
> **>>Therapist:** "I hear that very clearly, and I really do understand. But I also can't ignore the fact that you just mentioned another feeling, a feeling that you really wanted to do something else *[therapist now points to the spot to Nicky's right]*. And that's a different perspective – you sound different, you want different things. Both perspectives are there, they just aren't identical – they really are different feelings and perspectives. Does that seem right, if I put it that way?"
>
> **>>Nicky:** "Yes, that's right, yes…"

2.2.3 Step 3: Rationale for the technique

Now that the client's modes are associated with chairs, the chair exercise can be introduced (see table 2.2). This can be done simply by designating it as a standard exercise in the analysis phase. However, the introduction can also be tailored to the specific trigger of that moment, such as the internal conflict the client has just told you about or the experience that the client seems stuck in.

Table 2.2: Introducing the chair technique	
Pre-planned	"Today, I want us to do an exercise where I'll to ask you to sit in different chairs. This may seem a bit odd, but it will help us gain more insight into your problems and the reasons why you tend to get stuck."

Internal conflict	"It sounds like you're struggling; I hear two different experiences that you're caught up in. That internal conflict is now happening in your head. Let's do an exercise in which we make that internal conflict more visible here in the therapy room, so we can both look at it from a bit more of a distance."
Stuck in an experience	"I hear how you're completely full of this feeling *[e.g. of shame, guilt, fear, lack of feeling]*. As that experience is so strong, let's give it a literal, physical place in the room. So I'll pull up another chair, and that will be the place from which you can talk about this feeling."

In general, the recommendation is not to try to explain too much about chairwork to the client beforehand. After all, the purpose of the exercise is to generate an emotional experience that can be considered and reflected on in detail afterwards. On the other hand, chairwork can seem strange and uncomfortable to clients at first, and this is often experienced as a barrier (see Chapter 1). You can therefore explain that the use of chairs is a proven tool in which the client sits on a different chair to speak from the perspective that is the subject of discussion, and that its purpose is to gain insight into different experiences and the dynamics between them. You can emphasise that the client can stop the exercise at any time, but experience and research have shown that it is worth trying. For most clients, this is enough for them to be willing to start the exercise.

Introducing chairwork – Nicky

>>**Therapist:** "I want to do an exercise with chairs. That means I'll bring in an extra chair in a moment and ask you to sit there. You might wonder why we're going to play this game of 'musical chairs'?"

>>**Nicky:** *[hesitantly]* "Yes, well kind of, yes..."

>>**Therapist:** "Well, you've already seen me gesturing like this when we talk about your experiences. That on one side *[therapist gestures to Nicky's right]* you didn't want to go along, but on the other side *[gestures to Nicky's left]* you were so anxious about disappointing the others that you thought it would be better just to go along, to conform to their needs. That's right, isn't it?"

>>**Nicky:** "Yes, that's true..."

> **>>Therapist:** "So, there are two sides to your experience, and to you. And those chairs are going to help us separate those sides a bit more, here in the room, so we can get a better understanding of why they are there. That's how this chair technique can help us get more clarity on how to change things. I could tell you more about it, but I think the best way to find out how it works is just to give it a try. If you don't want to then you don't have to, or you want to stop the exercise at any time you can do that. But research and experience have shown that this exercise can be very effective. Would you like to give it a try? Then we can always discuss any questions you have afterwards."
>
> **>>Nicky:** "Alright..."

What if…

…the client has lots of questions about the technique?

Should this happen, you can compliment the client on his or her interest, interpreting the questions as a sign of positive curiosity about the technique rather than resistance (even if you don't feel this perception is strictly accurate). Then, one frequently asked question can be answered as follows:

>>Client: "Why do I have to sit in another chair? Can't I just talk about it from this chair?"
>>Therapist: "First of all, you don't have to do anything, it isn't compulsory. But it's a way of working that can really help us – research shows this, and I've also seen it myself. And of course, you can also talk about that experience from this chair. But this technique is actually meant to go a step beyond 'talking about' and give a better understanding from both perspectives involved in this conflict. That means we can take the path of 'feeling' more than the path of 'thinking'."

What if…

…the client is resistant?

The language of modes helps therapists to see resistance as a side of the client, not the whole client. The resistance is probably a Protector who is unwilling to give up control. Think of the discussion you have with the client more as a negotiation with that Protector – as if you're talking to a gatekeeper who isn't inclined to let you in. In that negotiation a calm tone, reassurance and explicitly mentioning that the client remains in control are the best strategies to secure agreement to try the technique. Another option is to actually make use of chairwork for the negotiation! You can ask the client to explain from another chair why it seems better not to do the technique, and in this way chairwork is introduced through the very mechanism of discussing the client's resistance to it.

What if…

…the client has strong resistance ("This is stupid, I'm not doing it!")?

This situation is particularly challenging because strong resistance can trigger feelings of uncertainty or anger in the therapist. However, the fact that the client has such a strong aversion to the technique does not mean that it was wrong to suggest it. Ultimately, all your conversations are intended to help the client, whether through seemingly odd techniques or not. So, for clients who are especially resistant to the idea of chairwork, this could be your possible response:

>>**Therapist:** "I can understand your reaction – this technique is a bit odd, like 'musical chairs'. So on the one hand, I'm now thinking *should I leave it out, since it's clear he isn't interested in it?* But on the other hand, I also think *odd or not, experience and research have shown that the technique can be very effective – and it would be a shame to miss out on something that could help him.* You know, I take you and your difficulties very seriously and want to do as much as I can to help you. And yes, I'd rather do something that seems a bit strange at first glance, but which could help you, than give up on it just because it seems silly. I think you and this therapy are too important for that. Could we just give it a try, and then discuss afterwards whether it helped us or not?"

2.2.4 Step 4: Have the client sit on another chair

Arriving at this point, you and your client have discovered and agreed that there are different sides, or modes, to their experience, and you have discussed chairwork as a good way to investigate those different sides. The time has come to add an extra chair to the therapy: "Now I'd like to ask you to sit on this chair here. Let's call it the chair for that side of you that feels you have to conform."

You are free to determine the position of the chair in the therapy room. However, it is good to be consistent with the positioning of chairs during the therapy. For example, if you have defined a mode while pointing to a spot to the client's right, you should ideally place the corresponding chair in the same spot and maintain that placement in subsequent sessions. This consistent repetition links the experience to that spot, increasing the transparency and clarity of the technique.

Some chair positions will be more obvious than others due to the types of modes and the common dynamics between them springing from the historical context in which they developed. For instance, Protectors often emerge as an early survival response to critical, sometimes punitive messages from attachment figures. In that historical context, the Protector often stood between those figures and the emotional pain triggered by their critical messages. So in chairwork, this may mean placing the Protector's chair between the Vulnerable Child's chair and the Critical Parent's chair. If this isn't possible, you could ensure that the Critical Parent's chair is farther away than the Protector's chair.

What if…

…the client doesn't want to switch chairs?

Some clients have difficulty with emotionally oriented exercises, and the consequent resistance can make them reluctant to switch chairs. In such situations, chairwork can also be applied 'under the radar'. The patient remains in their original chair, but the therapist vividly describes how chairwork is done and adds additional chairs. In this way the client observes, from the sidelines, a multiple-chair analysis of their situation – and from this perspective he or she may also experience something of the technique's power, leading to a greater willingness to participate more actively next time.

What if…

…the client forgets which chair represents which mode?

It is not uncommon for clients (and sometimes even therapists…) to get confused about which chair represents which mode or experience. This is particularly common in the early stages of therapy as the client is new to chairwork, and the novelty can be distracting. Similarly, the therapist has not yet become deeply familiar with the different sides of the client, which can make remembering which chair represents which mode confusing. The best way to maintain or regain clarity is to summarise everything regularly at a calm pace. This means that the therapist will often repeat things, but doing so is more likely to add clarity to the exercise than to be annoying for the client.

2.2.5 Step 5: Interview the mode

At this stage of treatment, the likelihood is that it will not yet be fully clear which side of the client you are interviewing. While the explicit description of their experience may be enough for you to make an initial hypothesis about which mode you are interviewing, the aim of chairwork is precisely to gain more insight into the client's presenting mode. A hypothesis might be made as shown below:

| avoid, adapt, reverse → functional behaviour → coping mode (the Protector) |
| negative self-image → internalised critical self-evaluations → parent mode (the Critical Parent) |
| primary emotions → natural emotional responses → child modes (for example the Vulnerable Child) |

The mode you are interviewing has implications for the kind of questions that you will ask during the interview. For instance, you will mostly ask the Protector about its protective function and the danger that is feared if the Protector is let go. The Critical Parent will be asked about the reasons for their self-criticism. The child modes will mainly be asked to express the emotions being experienced. Possible questions that might be asked of each mode are shown below:

Coping mode (Protector):	"What makes it better to avoid/adapt/fight?" "What could go wrong if you didn't avoid/adapt/fight?" "How long have you been there?"
Parent mode (Critical Parent):	"So what don't you like about what she/he did?" "So what do you think of her/him?"
Child mode (e.g. the Vulnerable Child):	"What are you sad/afraid/angry about?"

Give your client clear instructions about what to do during the exercise. Instead of saying: "Can you say a bit more about that avoidance tendency?", it is better to say: "Now crawl all the way into that state of mind in which you think avoidance is the best thing to do. Be that Avoider, and I'll speak to you as that Avoider. Tell me, Avoider, why do you think avoidance is the best approach?" From this point on, you are no longer talking indirectly about experiences or modes – instead, the client is addressed as the mode itself. Exploring the mode in this way takes the form of a sort of interview.

> ### Interviewing the mode – Nicky
>
> **>>Therapist:** "Well, I heard from Nicky *[using client's name and gesturing to the original (empty) chair]* that she would have preferred to stay home that day. But I understand that you *[gesturing to Nicky sitting in the other chair]* thought it would be better to go along, to conform to the needs and wishes of others, is that right?"
>
> **>>Nicky:** "Yes, it is."
>
> **>>Therapist:** "And in your opinion *[gesturing to Nicky]*, what is better about conforming to others' wishes than doing what Nicky *[gesturing to the original chair]* wanted?"
>
> **>>Nicky:** "Well, they were so excited about a plan – and they really wouldn't have liked it if I hadn't gone with them, you know..."
>
> **>>Therapist:** "And what do you think would have happened if you hadn't been there? What if Nicky had just done what she wanted *[gesturing to the original chair]* and stayed home?
>
> **>>Nicky:** "Well, I don't know, but I think they wouldn't have liked it and they might have been disappointed, and then they wouldn't invite me in the future or something like that..."

What if...

...the client thinks the interviewing is weird and doesn't go along with it?

Almost every client has some difficulty making the transition from reflecting about their overall situation to interviewing a specific mode. Clients have a tendency to keep speaking in general terms. For example, the therapist asks: "What made it seem better to you *[gesturing to the client in the Protector's chair]* to go along than for her *[gesturing to the empty chair where client was just sitting]* to say she'd rather stay home?" In the early exercises, many clients will give answers like, "Well, I did want to stay at home, but I also thought they'd be disappointed. And then I thought: 'I don't really feel like it, but I feel even less like dealing with drama'." With this kind of answer, they continue to identify with the different perspectives in the internal struggle, while the purpose of the exercise is precisely to separate them. You can help your client by rephrasing their answers each time in terms of the modes. By doing this several times, the client learns to think in terms of modes themselves.

> **Separating modes – Nicky**
>
> **>>Nicky:** "Well, I did want to stay at home, but I also thought they would be disappointed. And then I thought, 'I don't really feel like it, but I feel even less like dealing with drama'."
>
> **>>Therapist:** "So she [gesturing to the empty chair where Nicky was just sitting] wanted to stay home but you [gesturing to Nicky in the Protector's chair] were worried they would be disappointed?"
>
> **>>Nicky:** "Yes."
>
> **>>Therapist:** "And what were you afraid that others would think of her if you didn't go along with them?"
>
> **>>Nicky:** "I don't know... that she's boring or something."

The wording used by the client at this point in the example interview ("that she's boring") is positive, indicating that she is beginning to adopt the language of modes and to separate states of mind.

2.2.6 Step 6: Add a further chair or chairs for any other modes

So far, one extra chair has been added and, after interviewing the identified mode, the client can be asked to return to the original therapy chair. For example, on the extra chair the client might have spoken as the Vulnerable Child about the fear, sadness or loneliness they experienced in that mode. Back in the original therapy chair, you can reflect on those feelings together with the client.

You can, however, work with multiple chairs to gain more insight into the dynamics of the different modes. When multiple modes are found to be activated, you can add multiple chairs and the chair exercise becomes a multiple chair exercise. For instance, you may have interviewed the client's Critical Parent, but then find you want to know what feelings this mode evokes.

In this situation, you can then place a second chair for the Vulnerable Child opposite the Critical Parent, ask the client to sit on this new chair and then interview the client's emotional side before completing the exercise.

It is not always clear to clients what is expected of them when they move to a new chair, and they may need clear directions. For this reason, begin with a summary of what was said in the previous chair. By gesturing to the empty chair in which the interview just took place, the link between that experience and that location is reinforced once again. This can be further supported by personifying the experience in that chair – giving the modes a name, and using words like 'he' or 'she'.

> ### Establishing the client in a new chair and mode – Nicky
>
> **>>Therapist:** "So, what this Pleaser is saying *[gesturing to the empty chair where Nicky was just sitting]* is that it's best to go along with the others. Her fear *[gesturing again to the empty chair]* is that if she doesn't conform, they'll stop liking you *[now gesturing to Nicky]*. Do I have that right?"
>
> **>>Nicky:** "Yes..."
>
> **>>Therapist:** *[Leaning towards Nicky and using a soft voice]* "In this chair where you're sitting now, I want to ask you to make contact with the fear that this Pleaser *[gesturing towards the previous chair]* is talking about. What's so scary to you about others not liking you anymore?"

Instead of one extra chair, two chairs are now involved in the technique. You could even expand this with a third seat for the Protector. However, the analysis phase is intended to generate insights, and using multiple chairs can sometimes become confusing for your client. Because of this, in the early chair exercises in the analysis phase, the work is usually done with one or at most two chairs.

What if…

…a large number of different modes seem to have been activated?

It is not uncommon that multiple modes are activated in a given situation. For instance, the client feels vulnerable (the Vulnerable Child), and therefore starts to avoid (the Avoidant Protector). This avoidance activates self-criticism from the parent mode (Punitive Parent), but this itself provokes anger at the injustice of that self-criticism (the Angry Child). This causes the client to retreat into a sulky, antagonistic, irritable attitude (the Angry Protector), but in turn to feel bad about it (reactivating the Punitive Parent, which in turn reactivates the Vulnerable Child).

It would be possible to represent all these experiences with chairs and to make the internal dynamics visible that way. At this stage of therapy, however, when the client is first introduced to chairwork, there is a risk that so many different chairs would make the exercise too cluttered. For this reason, it is better to simplify the model. This means that some aspects of the situation may not be addressed, or may be discussed in a simpler, more clustered form. For instance, avoidance and irritable withdrawal can be framed simply as 'The Protector' using different forms of coping.

Note: The analysis phase involves only assessment, not treatment

Exploring modes in the analysis phase gives more insight into a client's experience. For instance, perhaps in the Protector mode, your client seems to believe that feelings are bad and dangerous and there is no benefit to them. Or, in the Critical Parent mode, your client feels the need to 'put on airs' when he or she feels anxious or sad. Your natural response as a care provider might be to respond with "Yes, but..." when you hear the Protector say it is particularly important not to listen to one's own needs or feelings, or when you hear the Critical Parent list all the things that are wrong with the client. However, in this exploratory phase the aim is to obtain information; as yet we are not seeking to change perspectives. A problem can only be solved effectively when it is well understood. For this reason, it is better to adopt an attitude in this interview that you just want to understand.

2.2.7 Step 7: Back to the original chair and reflection

After interviewing the different perspectives, you can reflect on the information that the exploration has yielded. This reflection can be done from the original chair. In this way, the 'therapy chair' becomes a place for the client's Healthy Adult, who learns to become aware of their different sides and eventually also how to handle them.

> ### Leaving the mode behind on the chair – Nicky
>
> **>>Therapist:** "I understand it's unpleasant to feel this fear, but I'm glad you shared it with me. I also think I understand better now why the Pleaser *[gesturing to the Pleaser's chair]* took over in that situation. I want to take a look with you at everything we've done and what we've learned. I'll ask you to go back to your original chair in a moment *[gesturing to the original therapy chair]*. When you get up from this chair *[gesturing to the chair where Nicky is still sitting]*, I want you to leave the fear we just talked about behind – this is the chair where you feel that fear, but it will be left behind on the chair when you get up. Please sit on this chair now *[gesturing to the original therapy chair]*.
>
> **>>Nicky:** "Okay." *[Nicky sits down on the original therapy chair.]*
>
> **>>Therapist:** "And in this chair, I'll speak to you as the Healthy Adult that you are. I'd like you to look back at those different experiences together with me from this chair *[gesturing to the chair where Nicky is sitting now]*. Who was sitting there again?" *[therapist gestures to Pleaser's chair.]*

An alternative is to ask the client to come and stand next to you. Standing side by side, you can walk past the different chairs and give a brief summary of the perspectives that were expressed in each one. Standing up is a physical movement that allows the client to detach a little more from the chair exercise. It also provides a physical position that gives an elevated overview, raising oneself above the concrete experiences. This makes it a good position for the Healthy Adult you are addressing in this reflection. Moreover, standing side by side symbolically reinforces the teamwork that takes place in this phase – trying to understand together what is going on within the client. Choosing whether to reflect on an exercise while standing can be a matter of taste for the therapist. However, it is a good option for those clients who have difficulty distancing themselves from their modes, and who continue to lapse into identifying with the experiences explored in the chairs.

> ### Reflecting from a standing position – Nicky
>
> **>>Therapist:** "Good, then I'd like to ask you now to get up from that chair and stand here with me."
>
> *[The therapist also stands and takes a position a few metres from the chairs used in the exercise. Nicky gets up a little hesitantly and stays next to her chair for a while at first.]*

> **>>Therapist:** "Just come and stand here next to me. Yes, I know, I'll show you every corner of the room. I want to look with you, from a distance, back at what we've just done. Now we're looking from a height at the empty chairs where you were just sitting. And what was the experience in this chair here again?" *[The therapist points to the Protector's chair.]*
>
> **>>Nicky:** "There I described that I just went with them after all…"
>
> **>>Therapist:** "Exactly. The Pleaser sits there, focusing on what others want and adjusting to it. And who was sitting there again?" *[The therapist now points to the Vulnerable Child's chair.]*
>
> **>>Nicky:** "That anxious one… afraid they'd be disappointed if I didn't go along."

Moving chairs to amplify dynamics and increase understanding

From this standing position, where everything can be surveyed, it is also easier to shift the chairs to make the mutual dynamics between the different sides even more clearly visible. For example, the Protector's chair can be moved in front of the Vulnerable Child's chair, illustrating the Protector's guarding function. Within this discussion, possible goals of therapy can also be considered.

> ### Moving chairs to amplify dynamics and increase understanding – Nicky
>
> **>>Therapist:** *[looks attentively at the chairs with Nicky]* "Yes… so I can see that the Pleaser, in trying to help and protect her *[pointing to the Vulnerable Child's chair]*, actually takes over, so that others don't get to see that she *[pointing to the Vulnerable Child]* has other needs that are not being met. *[The therapist, while talking, slides the Pleaser's chair in front of the Vulnerable Child's chair, so that the latter is somewhat hidden behind the Pleaser.]* Does that make sense at all?"
>
> *[Nicky nods.]*
>
> **>>Therapist:** "And if we look at it this way, from a bit of a distance, what do we really think about this? Do we think this Pleaser needs to get even better at pleasing others so she *[pointing at the Vulnerable Child]* is kept even better hidden?"
>
> **>>Nicky:** "No… no, that doesn't work… I've always done that, but it doesn't work."
>
> **>>Therapist:** "No, I can understand that. On the other hand, it doesn't seem right to me either to just say, 'Put the Pleaser aside right now' *[therapist moves the Pleaser's chair quite far away]* because that seems too vulnerable to me, too threatening for your vulnerable side."

> [Nicky nods in agreement.]
>
> **>>Therapist:** "But what if this Pleaser, in the session with me, did step aside just once in a while, like today? *[The therapist moves the Pleaser's chair to the side slightly, so a little bit of the Vulnerable Child's chair becomes visible.]* Then we'll be able to look for other ways to help her together *[pointing to the Vulnerable Child's chair]*. How does that sound to you?"
>
> **>>Nicky:** "Yes… it's a lot, but I do think that would be good, yes."

2.2.8 Step 8: Homework

If all goes well, the chairwork exercise will have provided all kinds of valuable and helpful insights. Although they have already been reflected on (in Step 7), and you have made regular summaries, these insights are likely to be forgotten without further repetition. It is therefore important that, for homework between sessions, the client regularly repeats the insights gained. A photo of the chairs can be a useful way to support this homework. The different modes can also be drawn on the board along with their characteristics (thoughts, feelings and behaviour) – a mode model. A photo of that mode model contains even more information than a photo of the chairs. You can ask the client to look at these photos each evening, and to consider which modes they have recognised in themselves over the course of the day. For example, the photos can be used when filling in diary forms as an exercise in recognising the modes that have been activated (see Van Genderen & Arntz, 2021, pp. 33-47). You can also ask the client to choose chairs at home to symbolise the different modes.

What if…

…at the next session, you find that the client has not completed the homework?

There are several possible explanations as to why a client may not do the homework between sessions. The homework assignment might not have been clear enough, or the exercise may still feel sufficiently uncomfortable that the client avoided it, consciously or otherwise. Another explanation may be that a client does not possess enough chairs to represent the different modes. If that is the case, then other symbolic representations can be used – such as different cushions on a sofa.

2.3 Chapter summary

This chapter has described a step-by-step plan that can be used as a guideline for chairwork in the analysis phase. Chairwork is an integral part of the analysis phase. Situations that lend themselves well to a chair exercise are an internal conflict within the client, or when the client is stuck in an experience. Explicitly defining and naming that experience, with the support of gestures, is the prelude to an exercise in which the client is asked to speak from different experiences in different chairs. Chairwork thus offers an opportunity to interview the different sides of the client in order to gain more insight into their different emotional experiences and the dynamics between them.

The biggest pitfall when conducting chairwork is the client talking too cognitively about experiences, instead of viewing them from within the different perspectives themselves. As a therapist, you should therefore provide clear direction and instructions. The exercise concludes with a reflection on what information and insights into the dynamics between the client's different modes it has produced. For this reason, it is also important that the client repeats the insights gained regularly between sessions and learns to recognise the different sides of themselves. Recognising modes is the first step towards influencing and changing them. The next chapter describes how chairwork can be used to influence modes within the initial phase of therapy.

Chapter 3: The initial phase of therapy

Chapter 3: The initial phase of therapy

Chapter map	
3.1	Introduction
3.2	General guidelines for using chairwork
3.3	Chairwork with a Protector in the initial phase
3.4	Chairwork with a Critical Parent in the initial phase
3.5	Chairwork with the Vulnerable Child
3.6	Chairwork with the Angry Child
3.7	Chairwork with the Healthy Adult
3.8	Chapter summary

3.1 Introduction

Once the analysis phase is completed, the actual schema therapy treatment and process of change begins. This focuses on breaking or changing patterns of symptoms, and it consists of an initial phase, a middle phase and a final phase. Each phase has its own objectives and characteristics, and chairwork will be done differently in each of them. There are two main objectives in the initial phase of schema therapy – firstly learning to become more aware of activated modes, and secondly gaining corrective emotional experiences. Chairwork is an important tool for achieving both.

For example, a recent problem situation can be explored using chairwork to identify different modes. This resembles the use of chairwork in the analysis phase, where symptoms and situations were also being explored. However, unlike in the analysis phase, a mode model is now in place, the client's different sides can be referred to more quickly, and chairwork can therefore focus more on exploration than discovery. After all, while the modes may now have been identified, at this stage they are often still only theoretical concepts for the client and chairwork can help to achieve more experiential recognition of them.

Achieving corrective emotional experiences is more complex, as in the initial phase you cannot call on the healthy side of the client. Frequently this mode is not yet strong enough to create such experiences by itself, and so the therapist needs to have an active, guiding role when implementing chair exercises.

This chapter provides detailed information on how to apply chairwork with coping, parent and child modes, and how to include the client's Healthy Adult mode within chairwork at an early stage of therapy – even if that side is not yet well-developed. Before explaining the chair technique for each mode individually, some more general guidance is given for applying chairwork effectively. These guidelines summarise and extend the steps that were described in Chapter 2.

3.2 General guidelines for using chairwork

3.2.1 Use of gestures in preparation for chairwork

It is not self-evident to clients that they have different sides to themselves. You must teach the client to think in terms of modes not only by identifying and *naming* modes, but also by giving each one more form by pointing to a specific place in the room when naming it. In this way, that place is linked to a specific mode – and placing a chair in that same spot will be a logical prelude to chairwork.

3.2.2 Reformulations in mode language

In the early stages of exercises, you will regularly need to rephrase the client's statements as if they were emanating directly from the modes. Doing this teaches your client to distinguish the different sides of their experience better.

> Using gestures and reformulations – Nicky
>
> **>>Therapist:** "In this chair, I'd like to ask you to talk about the criticism you have of her *[gesturing to the original chair]*. So be that critical voice. Now, what do you *[gesturing to Nicky]* think is wrong with her *[gesturing to the original chair]* idea of staying home, even though others want to go out?"
>
> **>>Nicky:** "I just shouldn't be so difficult about it. After all it's nice that they want us all to do some**thing together, and then I'll just stay home for a bit!**"

>>**Therapist:** "Okay, so you *[gesturing to the client]* think she *[gesturing to the original chair]* is making things difficult when she makes her own plans instead of going along with what others expect of her? What do you think of her – of her wanting to make her own plans?"

>>**Nicky:** "It's just not nice. I don't know, I guess I'm stupid or stubborn, difficult… it makes me feel like a bit of a killjoy."

>>**Therapist:** "So if she *[gesturing to the original chair]* doesn't want to go out with the others, you *[gesturing to the client]* think she's being a killjoy, being difficult?"

3.2.3 Use of non-verbal and paralinguistic communication

Although the specific method of questioning/interviewing may differ by mode, the actual questions can sometimes still be the same. For example, the question "What are you afraid will happen if you don't do what others want?" can be used to explore the Vulnerable Child's primary feelings, and also to investigate the function of the Protector. However, remember that you are interviewing a side of the client, a mode of being, and not just the cognitive content of the experience. In other words, you are interviewing two different 'persons', and the style of interviewing will need to be adapted to the 'person' or side that is sitting opposite you. The actual questions you ask may be the same, but they are asked in a different tone of voice, at a different pace and with a different attitude. Exploring the Vulnerable Child's primary emotions, for example, involves a softer voice, more explicit understanding and more help – such as making suggestions when naming emotions. Exploring the Protector, by contrast, is accompanied by a sympathetic but more mature speaking tone, and allows more room for the Protector's autonomy and self-expression. And interviewing a Demanding Parent involves the same mature tone and attitude, but with less sympathy for that side's critical comments than for the Protector's guarding function.

3.2.4 Give clear directions

It helps clients if you are clear in your directions, especially when changing chairs. Moving from one chair to another represents a transition from one state of mind (mode) to another. Although it is simple enough for clients to physically change chairs, switching between states of mind is often more complex. To support the transition from the old chair to the new one, and with it to a different emotional state of mind and experience, clear instructions are needed from you as the therapist.

> **Giving clear directions before changing chairs – Nicky**
>
> **>>Therapist:** "Okay, in a moment I'll ask you to get up from your chair. But before you do, I want you to be aware that the place where you're sitting now is the Pleaser's chair. On this chair, it's fine to talk about why adapting to others is the best thing you can do. But once you stand up, I want you to leave that perception in the chair, as if it was stuck to the seat with Super Glue. So just take a moment to let that sink in, and then I'll ask you to get up from that chair and sit here next to me."

3.2.5 Provide regular summaries

In the initial phase of therapy, and often beyond, the client will still regularly lose track of all the different modes and chairs. Regular summaries may feel like unnecessary repetition to you as a therapist, but in practice they often prove indispensable in offering the client clear and sustained insight into the different modes that exist and the dynamics between them.

> **Repeating and recapping – Nicky**
>
> **>>Therapist:** "Okay, so there *[gesturing to the Protector's spot]* is that Pleaser who thinks it's better for you to adapt around what others want. But you *[gesturing to the client on the other chair]* would have preferred something else, right?"
>
> **>>Nicky:** "Yes, I would have preferred just to stay at home."
>
> **>>Therapist:** "Okay, so you wanted to stay home but she *[gesturing to the Protector's chair]* thought it would be better to conform to the expectations of others."

3.3 Chairwork with a Protector in the initial phase

The Protector has a defensive and guarding function, with the aim of minimising underlying feelings of vulnerability, fear, sadness or anger. This mode also protects the client from negative messages springing from parent modes. The overwhelming emotional experiences of the Vulnerable Child can be held off using avoidance, surrender or inversion. As we noted in Chapter 2, the problem with clients' Protectors is not the mode per se – in a sense we all have one – but the fact that clients have no control over it. The aim of therapy is to access underlying emotions and needs by reducing the influence of the Protector, which means first making the client aware of it and secondly negotiating a way past it. There are several ways in which chairwork can be applied with a Protector in the initial phase of therapy. However, for therapists who aren't yet experienced with the technique, the step-by-step plan shown below can be useful. As experience and confidence grows, so will your repertoire.

Step-by-step plan for chairwork with a Protector in the initial phase of therapy
Step 1: Recognise the Protector
Step 2: Name the Protector
Step 3: Have the client sit on another chair
Step 4: Negotiate with the Protector
Step 5: Have the client sit on the chair of the Vulnerable Child
Step 6: Validate the relevant basic needs
Step 7: Have the client sit on the original chair (or stand with you) for summary and reflection
Step 8: Homework

3.3.1 Step 1: Recognise the Protector

The first step is for the client to recognise the Protector when it is active. A simple way to identify the Protector is to ask about the client's emotions and needs. An active Protector makes it difficult for the client to share their emotions openly and vulnerably. How the client responds to questioning about feelings may vary by type of Protector. A client with a Detached Protector, for example, is more likely to respond with 'I don't feel anything', while a client with a Self-Aggrandising Protector might respond with: 'I understand that you like to talk about feelings. But I'm really not comfortable sharing mine with a novice therapist.'

Although the responses vary, what all Protectors have in common is that they give away very little information about how the client actually feels. They often give short answers in which the client says they don't feel like sharing or don't see the point. There are also non-verbal and paralinguistic characteristics of Protectors, such as a lack of emotion in the voice or facial expression. Often the emotions displayed are variations of anger, rather than vulnerability such as sadness or fear.

As a therapist, you can also recognise a Protector by the effect that the mode has on how you yourself feel in this contact; for example, you feel emotionally disconnected and notice yourself becoming cautious or withdrawing. You can further recognise a Protector by contrasting it with the client's other states of mind during conversations. While it might be difficult to determine whether or not your client is in a Protector mode at any specific moment in time, often that state is clearly more emotionally closed in comparison to other periods in the conversation and session. Finally, there is of course the information from the analysis phase that helps to recognise this mode.

> ### Recognising the Protector – Nicky
>
> **>>Therapist:** "How have you been feeling over the past week?"
>
> **>>Nicky:** [with somewhat flat voice and not much facial expression] "Normal…"
>
> **>>Therapist:** "And how would you define that feeling, 'normal'?"
>
> **>>Nicky:** [looking away] "Well, just, I don't know… things are fine. I went to work, and it was fine."
>
> **>>Therapist:** "So you went to work, and it was fine, and how did that feel – good?"
>
> **>>Nicky:** "Well, good… like I said, normal. Nothing special."
>
> **>>Therapist:** "And how did it go at work?"
>
> **>>Nicky:** "Well, fine…"
>
> **>>Therapist:** "What do you want to discuss today?"
>
> **>>Nicky:** "I don't know… I don't really have anything."
>
> [At this point, the therapist may begin to feel uncomfortable, uncertain about how to proceed, and somewhat irritated that the client is not being more cooperative in the conversation.]

The literature on schema therapy, and the questionnaires used to identify modes, describe several variants of Protectors. An overview of these modes and their key features is given below.

Table 3.1: Overview of the different Protectors and their key features
1. Compliant Surrenderer[a]
In this mode, clients surrender to the will of others in order to avoid conflict or anticipated problems. They suppress their needs and emotions, often resulting in pent-up anger, and hope for approval by behaving submissively, passively and/or obediently. Clients in this mode run the risk of other people taking advantage of them.
2. Detached Protector[a]
In this mode, clients shield themselves from strong feelings, thinking that feelings are a sign of weakness or that they might be overwhelmed by them. In contact with others, they are distant and try to eliminate their feelings. They may feel empty, insensitive or as if they are 'outside' themselves. When clients become so detached that it is almost impossible to talk to them, this is called 'dissociation'. They may then experience emptiness, indifference and/or alienation.
3. Angry Protector[b]
In this mode, clients shield themselves from intense feelings and try to keep others at a distance by adopting an angry, cynical, pessimistic or dismissive attitude. They distrust others and exhibit anger to in order to protect themselves from perceived threats.
4. Detached Self-Soother[a]
In this mode, clients seek distraction in order to avoid having to feel negative emotions. They do this by using substances (drugs, alcohol) or engaging in stimulating activities (fanatically or excessively doing things like working, using the Internet, watching TV, gaming, gambling, sports or sex).
5. Perfectionistic Overcontroller[b]
In this mode, clients try to protect themselves against the possibility of making mistakes by being extremely perfectionist. They control themselves or others compulsively, work hard, and go to great lengths to do things as well as possible.
6. Suspicious Overcontroller[b]
In this mode, clients seek to protect themselves against the threat of other people by being extremely controlling of others and checking their intentions. In doing so, they look for confirmation of their suspicions.

7. Attention and Approval Seeker
In this mode, clients try to gain approval and attention from others in a flamboyant way – for example by exaggerating or eroticising their behaviour or emotions.
8. Self-Aggrandiser[a]
In this mode, clients feel superior to others and think they have special rights. They want to impose their will without having to consider others. They emphasise their own achievements and belittle those of others to increase their own self-esteem, or because they feel entitled to.
9. Bully and Attack[a]
In this mode, clients bully, intimidate or attack others in order to avoid being humiliated or hurt.
10. Conning and Manipulative[b]
In this mode, clients deceive, lie to or manipulate others in order to achieve certain goals, such as avoiding punishment or gaining an advantage for themselves.
11. Predator[b]
In this mode, clients are focused on eliminating a threat, obstacle, rival or enemy in a cold, ruthless and calculating way. They take revenge on others in an attempt to maintain their position, or because they feel that the other person is standing in their way.

[a] Included in the Schema Mode Inventory [SMI; Young, J., Arntz, A., Atkinson, T., Lobbestael, J., Weishaar, M., Vreeswijk, M.F., & Klokman, J. (2007). Schema Mode Inventory (SMI version 1). New York: Schema Therapy Institute]. For the description of modes, see also Rijkeboer, M., Van Genderen, H., & Arntz, A. (2017). *Schematherapie: theorie, praktijk en onderzoek*. In: Eurelings- Bontekoe, E.H.M., Verheul, R. & Snellen, W.M. (Ed.) *Handboek persoonlijkheidspathologie*. Houten: Bohn Stafleu van Loghum.

[b] Forensic modes as described by Bernstein, D.P., Keulen de Vos, M., & Arntz, A. (2007). Schema Focused Therapy in forensic settings: Theoretical model and recommendations for best clinical practice. *International Journal of Forensic Mental Health* **6** (2) 169–183.

What if…

…you are unsure whether the presenting mode is a Protector or not?

Sometimes, in spite of all the information and knowledge about the different modes you obtained in the analysis phase, it may still be unclear what mode or state of mind a client is in. In such situations, you can still start with chairwork and use the exercise partly as an analysis method. This may then gradually reveal whether or not the client's mode is indeed a Protector.

3.3.2 Step 2: Name and locate the Protector

Now that you have identified the Protector, the next step is to name it explicitly to the client. It could be a quite generic name, like the Pleaser (as in the example, where Nicky's Protector wants her to conform to the wishes of others), or a more personal name like Tough Tom. Giving the Protector a name helps the client to create more distance from it, making it almost a 'separate' person that can be spoken to. When doing this, go beyond words – also point the Protector out with gestures, almost as if pointing to someone else in the room. This will again make the transition to chairwork in the next step easier.

> **Locating the Protector – Nicky**
>
> **>>Therapist:** "I noticed that my questions about how you felt seemed to be difficult for you. Is that right? This isn't meant as a criticism at all, but I notice that it's easier for you to talk about what you did than to talk about how you felt... do you recognise that?"
>
> **>>Nicky:** "I don't know, there just isn't that much to tell. I just don't feel that much in particular."
>
> **>>Therapist:** "Exactly, I noticed. I know that you can feel a lot – you're actually quite an emotional person *[gesturing to a place to the right of the client]* but not today. As you're sitting there now *[gesturing to a place to the left of the client]*, you don't seem to feel much. Last time, I saw much more of your emotional side *[gesturing again to the client's right]*, but when I ask about your feelings now, it's more difficult because as you're sitting there *[gesturing again to the client's left]*, you don't feel much. Does that sound right at all?"
>
> **>>Nicky:** "Yes, I don't know why that is either, it's just quieter."
>
> **>>Therapist:** "I'm sure there must be a reason why you're in that state of not feeling *[gesturing again to the client's left]*. Shall we do an exercise that can help us understand better why that is?"

3.3.3 Step 3: Have the client sit on another chair

At this point, your client's Protector has been named and you can ask if the client wants to sit on another chair. An explanation of the purpose and usefulness of chairwork has already been given in the analysis phase, and you shouldn't need to repeat it now unless the client asks. You should place an extra chair in the spot you pointed at when you were talking about the client's Protector.

You might wonder, or your client might wonder, why the Protector should be placed in a different chair. Wouldn't it be easier to let the client stay where they are and simply call that the Protector's chair? If you did this, you could skip a step of the exercise so that you could progress more smoothly. However, there are a few reasons why it is still better to place the Protector on a separate chair. First, by providing a specific Protector chair, the original therapy chair remains available as the chair for the client's Healthy Adult. Moving to another chair also sends an implicit message from the therapist that the Protector will eventually have to step aside. Finally, the physical change of position contributes to the feeling of being released from the Protector mode.

In your instructions to your client, be clear about what to do next. It might feel uncomfortable telling the client what they 'must' do, but clarity now will help you both in the longer term.

> ### Having the client sit in another chair – Nicky
>
> **>>Therapist:** "Let's do an exercise that can help us understand better why you're in this closed-off state. Please sit on the chair beside you now."
>
> *[Nicky sits on the chair that has been added.]*
>
> **>>Therapist:** "Okay, in this chair I'd like to ask you to be that 'non-feeling' Nicky. That shouldn't be too hard, because you were already kind of in that state of mind, right?"
>
> *[Nicky nods.]*
>
> **>>Therapist:** "Just be the 'non-feeler' here. And I'll also talk to you like that. I feel like today it might be more comfortable for you to be in that state instead of one where you feel a lot, do you agree?"
>
> **>>Nicky:** "Yes, of course."
>
> **>>Therapist:** "How would she *[gesturing to the spot to the left of the therapy chair]* feel if you weren't there?"

What if...

...the client doesn't see the point of the exercise and wants to know what it is good for?

Firstly, it is worth remembering that your client is in the Protector mode and questions are therefore likely to be asked from that state of mind. This means that you are not dealing with a hesitant or poorly motivated client as much as a protective gatekeeper who is reluctant to grant you access to the client's hidden emotional side. In fact, this metaphor of a gatekeeper can be useful in helping to motivate the client to do the exercise. Other arguments you can bring into this initial negotiation are:

- "I've personally found this to be a very useful exercise, and it is also supported by research."
- "If we have a better understanding of why you became closed-off, we'll also be better at looking for alternatives."
- "The best way to experience how useful the exercise can be is by doing it."
- "You are always in control, and you can decide to stop the exercise at any time."

3.3.4 Step 4: Negotiate with the Protector

As noted above, you can think of the Protector as a gatekeeper who keeps the gate to the client's Vulnerable Child closed. There are different types of Protectors, and therefore different gatekeepers that you might be confronted with as a therapist. Whatever type of gatekeeper you find in front of you, the best strategy to get the gate open is not to try to break through it, but to persuade the gatekeeper to grant you access. This means that you need to use some form of negotiation. There are different ways to approach this, but some common elements are always included:

- Explore the benefits of the Protector.
- Discuss the disadvantages of the Protector.
- Ask permission to contact the Vulnerable Child, offering reassurance, control and hope.

Element 1: Explore the benefits of the Protector

The Protector has in the past been functional in the context in which it was formed. Even in the client's current life, the Protector still offers many short-term benefits. For example, avoiding contact with others, or indeed conforming to others, has the short-term benefit of making the client feel less anxious. Expressing recognition and understanding of those benefits will make your client feel understood, which increases the likelihood that he or she will want to open up to you. Too many therapists tend to be quick to point to the disadvantages of the Protector by saying "Yes, but…". Take time to discuss the Protector's benefits, and be explicitly understanding with statements like:

- "Yes, I understand that. It actually sounds very reasonable to keep all those feelings away from her *[gesturing to the place next to the original therapy chair]*, because of course it's quite uncomfortable to feel all that."
- "Yes, I understand that very well. I could see myself doing the same, pushing those feelings of fear and sadness away *[gesturing to the spot to the left of the original therapy chair]* so as to be able to keep functioning."
- "I'm glad you're here *[gesturing to the client in the Protector's chair]*, because otherwise she *[gesturing to the spot to the left of the therapy chair]* would have had a much harder time than she's having now."

By validating the benefits of the Protector explicitly, you are not so much reinforcing the Protector as showing understanding for the reasons why it is active. You can trust that the disadvantages of the Protector will also be discussed, and that they will soon outweigh the benefits.

Element 2: Discuss the disadvantages of the Protector

When moving on to discuss the disadvantages of the Protector, ask first about the ways in which the Protector keeps feelings at a distance. Although you have already uncovered information about this in the analysis phase, the question can be a good entry point for discussing the ways in which the Protector does not help the client in the long term. After discussing how the Protector tries to keep emotions away as much as possible, you can ask how successful that behaviour is:

- "And what happens to those feelings when you find distraction/don't think about it/lose yourself in work/etc.? Do those feelings then get resolved?"
- "Are you happy if you find distraction/don't think about it/lose yourself in work/etc.?"
- "Do you feel positive emotions when you try so hard to avoid/suppress those feelings?"

With such questions, the long-term disadvantages of the Protector quickly come to the fore.

> ### Demonstrating the Protector's disadvantages – Nicky
>
> **>>Therapist:** "Okay, so you protect her *[gesturing to the spot to the left of the original therapy chair]* by just keeping all those feelings away, by concentrating on other things and by not talking about it. I can understand why you'd try to keep those feelings away if they bother you so much – I also have a protective side that tries to keep fear or sadness away. But what happens to her emotions when you do that? Does pushing them away help to solve them?"
>
> **>>Nicky:** "No... not really, well at least in that moment it does, but I might feel the same again later."
>
> **>>Therapist:** "Okay... so you can give her protection in the moment itself, by seeking distraction or getting absorbed in work, but it's not as if those feelings are resolved. So you aren't a real solution, are you, no matter how well you can protect her from those feelings within those moments?"

Element 3: Ask permission to make contact with the Vulnerable Child, offering reassurance, control and hope

You can now ask permission to make contact with the client's Vulnerable Child. From the Protector's perspective, you are asking for the gates to be thrown open, to admit possible hurt and pain. To address this, offer hope, reassurance and control. Reinforce that you want to offer a positive experience that is different from the one that the client is familiar with, and emphasise that the Protector remains in control and they can stop the exercise at any time if they want to.

> ### Asking the Protector's permission – Nicky
>
> **>>Therapist:** "Okay, so you're very good at protecting her from that sadness in the moment, but this doesn't resolve those feelings – it just pushes them away temporarily. I think we can do more. I think I can actually help her to feel better. How does that sound to you?"
>
> **>>Nicky:** "Well... great, but I can't really imagine it."
>
> **>>Therapist:** "I understand. It sounds impossible? I'd like to have the opportunity to prove to you that it can be done – that those feeling of sadness can be overcome – but I need your cooperation. If you'll give me the chance, I'd like to get in contact with her and let her know that there are other options besides just pushing away sadness and fear. Could you let me try? You can always step in if you want to stop – you're the one in control."
>
> **>>Nicky:** "I don't know... I still have to go to work after this, and I'm really not going to manage that if I start feeling as sad as I did the other day."

> **Therapist:** "I honestly think the exercise will make you feel better; at least that's what I'll try my very best to achieve. But if it puts your mind at ease, I can promise that I'll make sure you're in charge again well before the end of the session. And I honestly think that will be easy; you've been there as a Protector for so long that you're very good at what you do – finding distractions, pushing away feelings. You've had almost a lifetime of training in that. If 'keeping feelings away' was an Olympic event, you'd be in the running for a medal. So I think you can put some trust in that; it will be harder to get you to step aside than to let you take the wheel again. What do you think?"

3.3.5 Step 5: Have the client sit on the chair of the Vulnerable Child

If the client agrees, you should now take out a second chair and place it in the spot designated for the Vulnerable Child. Alternatively, you can ask the client to return to the original chair if that is where you wish them to connect with the Vulnerable Child. Either way, once the client is seated, ask them to connect with their feelings and needs. Sometimes those feelings will already have arisen spontaneously while you were talking about whether to do the exercise, or after you said you wanted to help them. Still, connecting with the Vulnerable Child can represent a major transition for your client. For this reason it is important to support the transition by giving clear instructions, keeping the pace slow, and regularly providing summaries and paraphrasing. The transition from chair to chair, and from mode to mode, can be facilitated by the positioning of the chairs, with the Vulnerable Child sitting closer to the therapist than the Protector. You can also support the transition with tone of voice – by speaking to the Vulnerable Child more softly and with more emotion than you did in the adult negotiation with the Protector.

> ### Transitioning between chairs and modes – Nicky
>
> **Therapist:** "Okay, I'm now going to ask you to get up from your chair and sit on the chair next to me. But do bear in mind that when you get up from that chair, the Protector stays there. Leave it stuck there while you come and sit here next to me."
>
> *[Nicky sits down on the designated chair next to the therapist.]*
>
> **Therapist:** *[softer voice]* "So there *[gesturing to the Protector's chair]* is the Protector who's trying to help you by pushing away all your sadness and fears. She does that by thinking about it as little as possible, by staying focused on work. But in the meantime, you feel sad, and you've also felt anxious over the past week. Can you tell me what made you so sad and anxious?"

3.3.6 Step 6: Validate the relevant basic needs

In your negotiation with the Protector, you promised to make the client feel better. This may sound ambitious, but in fact it is very attainable. To deliver on it, first show explicit compassion and understanding. The feeling of being seen and understood by someone else is a universal basic need that has a soothing effect on all of us; it works like a salve that helps to alleviate emotional pain. Compassion consists of the explicit expression of understanding – for the emotions related to the current situation, and also for the past emotional pain that is being re-activated in the present.

> ### Validating basic needs – Nicky
>
> **>>Therapist:** "When I listen to you, it doesn't seem strange to me at all that you felt sad and anxious. I think anyone in this situation *[gesturing to a place in front of Nicky]* would feel uncomfortable and find it difficult. So of course you feel sad and anxious. But when I think of you, I realise that you've experienced these kinds of situations and moments too often in your life – this is the umpteenth time that you've been alone and felt threatened. So of course you'll be completely out of sorts at that moment, because that old hurt from the past is coming back and playing a part."

Although showing compassion has a soothing effect in and of itself, it is still important to make your client explicitly aware of this effect. In the intensity of their emotions, clients tend to pay attention mainly to their pain and the situation that has made them feel so wretched. Explicitly directing their attention to the act and effect of compassion is a way to increase its impact.

> ### Highlighting compassion – Nicky
>
> **>>Therapist:** "How does it feel when you hear me say that it actually makes sense for you to feel that way? How does it feel to be understood like this? Is it a nice feeling *[the therapist holds his thumb up diagonally]* or not so nice *[moving thumb down a bit]*?"

What if…

…there is an Overcompensating Protector, and in this mode the client is being offensive and/or condescending about the compassion offered?

Clients are often unaccustomed to explicit compassion and recognition, and it may evoke an awkward, uncomfortable feeling. This can result in the client reverting to the Protector, and some Protectors can be strongly dismissive or even condescending. Firstly, it helps to realise that you are dealing with the protective side of your client in such moments. The appreciation that this is just one side of the client, not the whole client, can make challenging situations like this more manageable, especially if you use gestures that link the experience to the Protector's chair. It may sometimes be necessary to put the client back in the Protector's chair and renegotiate. Either way, you can calm the Protector by arguing that being unaccustomed to compassion does not mean that compassion is the problem; the client just has to get used to something new that will benefit them a great deal.

3.3.7 Step 7: Have the client sit on the original chair (or stand with you) for summary and reflection

Conclude the exercise by asking the client to get up from the Vulnerable Child's chair. If you have promised to put the Protector back in control by the end of the session, you can ask the client to take a seat in the Protector's chair again now. If that promise wasn't required, then you can just ask the client to return to the original therapy chair. In this chair, you summarise the exercise and speak to the client's Healthy Adult to reflect on the experience. Alternatively, you can ask to client to stand with you while you look down at the chairs, and in that position speak to their Healthy Adult.

Common conclusions arising from the negotiation with the Protector are that:

- The Protector was functional in the past and is still effective in the short term.
- The Protector is not a solution to the problems or feelings that are difficult for the client.
- Contact with the Vulnerable Child is painful in the short term.
- Recognition and compassion for those feelings has a healing effect.

3.3.8 Step 8: Homework

After reviewing and summarising, you then look ahead to the future: how will the client remember these reflections and experiences? What does the client want to take from this into the coming week, and what homework does he or she need to complete? Homework is given at the end of every session in order to ensure that the therapy has maximum effect; in the initial phase, it focuses mainly on repeating the conclusions from the exercise and recognising the Protector in everyday life.

3.4 Chairwork with a Critical Parent in the initial phase

A parent mode or Critical Parent is a state of mind in which clients judge themselves in the same way that they experienced important attachment figures judging them in the past. These internalised messages have contributed to their current symptom patterns. Therapy aims to reduce these messages and replace them with healthier self-assessments. Unlike Protectors, the strategy for working with parent modes in the initial phase is not to negotiate but to actively contradict or 'fight' those messages. This is because the assumptions of parent modes, unlike those of Protectors, are not functional or healthy at their core. Protectors can be understood as having good, protective intentions; however there is nothing healthy about modes which lead clients to see themselves as stupid, bad or worthless. Beliefs like these need to be replaced by more constructive self-assessments.

The somewhat dichotomous strategy of 'fighting' is deliberately chosen in the initial phase of therapy because the client's Healthy Adult mode is not yet sufficiently well-developed to integrate the nuances and complexities in their perceptions of the attachment figures. In the middle and final stages of treatment, by developing and strengthening the client's Healthy Adult, we will work towards a more nuanced view of the client. Chairwork at the beginning of therapy allows you to externalise and fight parent modes. In doing so, you can serve as a role model for a healthier adult self-assessment. Again, a step-by-step plan can provide guidance on how to perform the technique.

Step-by-step plan for chairwork with a Critical Parent in the initial phase of therapy
Step 1: Recognise the Critical Parent
Step 2: Name and locate the Critical Parent
Step 3: Have the client sit on another chair and interview the Critical Parent

Step 4: Have the client sit on the chair of the Vulnerable Child and offer care and compassion
Step 5: Fight the Critical Parent
Step 6: Check the effect of the intervention on the Vulnerable Child and offer care if necessary
Step 7: Have the client sit on the original chair (or stand with you) for summary and reflection
Step 8: Homework

3.4.1 Step 1: Recognise the Critical Parent

Chapter 1 described how to recognise and differentiate various modes. The most recognisable signs of a Critical Parent are briefly repeated below. This uses the following sources of information:

- Listen to *what* the client says.
- Listen to *how* the client says it.
- Listen to your own *countertransference response*.
- Note the *contrasts* in the client's presentation.

The client in a Critical Parent mode will make concrete, critical statements about themselves or their performance. This criticism can be heard in their tone of voice. For example, you can hear anger, but it is directed inward at the client, not outward. This can trigger a countertransference response in the therapist to counter it, because the criticism is often oversimplified and unreasonable.

> **Recognising the Critical Parent – Nicky**
>
> **>>Nicky:** "It's been a rubbish week. Everything went wrong, I did everything wrong. I always do everything wrong, I'm a complete failure!"
>
> **>>Therapist:** "Well, that sounds a bit strong, and I also disagree that you're a failure."
>
> **>>Nicky:** "That's because you don't really know me yet. If you did, you'd be fed up with me too. I'm slow and I make mistakes all the time, like this week. I just cause trouble for others."

> **>>Therapist:** "Is that true? Didn't your boyfriend say the other day that you make him very happy?"
>
> **>>Nicky:** "He only says that to avoid getting me more worked up; he doesn't mean anything by it."

Variations of the Critical Parent are described in the literature and questionnaires related to the different modes. The overview below shows the main characteristics of these parent modes.

Table 3.2: Parent mode types
1. Demanding Parent
In this mode, clients believe that they must do everything perfectly and should be capable of this. They must fulfil strict rules, norms and values. For example, they need to be overly efficient. They think they are never good enough and should try harder to do their best. Because of this, clients continue to strive for their high standards and perfection at the expense of their own peace of mind and pleasure. However, they are never satisfied with the results they achieve. This mode includes the internalised rules and norms of parents, other carers, educators, peers, culture or society.
2. Punitive Parent (variant: Guilt-Inducing Parent)
In this mode, clients relentlessly beat themselves up. They are angry with themselves for what they are doing or have done wrong, and they feel they should be punished harshly for it. This mode includes punitive messages received in the past from parents, educators or peers. A variation on the Punitive Parent is the Guilt-Inducing Parent, which unjustly makes clients feel very guilty.

3.4.2 Step 2: Name and locate the Critical Parent

Identify the Critical Parent by saying that the client seems to be looking at themselves in an angry, critical way, and should be given a name that is in keeping with this. Support this naming with gestures that indicate the Critical Parent's position for use in the chair exercise. Naming the mode is a form of metacommunication; you try to talk with the client about that critical self-assessment. However, clients will often respond from the Critical Parent's point of view, trying to convince you of the validity of the self-criticism. It is a trap to get involved with that conviction at this point in the exercise. Countering the Critical Parent is more effective when your client is more aware of that state of mind. Because of this, it is usually not enough to identify and name the Critical Parent only once – it will need to be repeated regularly until your client learns to recognise that state of mind.

> Locating the Critical Parent – Nicky
>
> **>>Therapist:** "Listening to you, it sounds as if you're not looking at yourself *[gesturing toward the client from a place opposite the client]* kindly, but with an angry and critical eye. Is that true?"
>
> **>>Nicky:** "But it's true, I mess everything up!"
>
> **>>Therapist:** "Exactly, that's what I notice, you sound angry while talking about yourself. I hear that punitive side *[gesturing to the spot opposite the client]* that mostly just sees and condemns mistakes. Does that sound right?"
>
> **>>Nicky:** "Yes, but isn't it stupid to keep making mistakes over and over again? This week…"
>
> **>>Therapist:** "Sorry to interrupt, but you asked me a question. I don't know if and what mistakes you made, but what I do notice, and what I want to reflect back to you, is that you seem to be looking at yourself from an angry, judgmental point of view *[again making a movement from a place opposite the client towards the client]*, and that sounds punitive. Is that so?"
>
> **>>Nicky:** "Yes, but it is true though…"
>
> **>>Therapist:** "That's just what I mean. You're so absorbed in that angry, judgmental perspective *[gesturing to the punitive place]* and so full of how much you've failed at everything, that it almost sounds strange when I talk about a 'punitive side' as a part of you, right?"
>
> **>>Nicky:** "Yes…"
>
> **>>Therapist:** "And that's exactly how it works. When that punitive side is in charge of you, you're in the midst of it and there's nothing else – you are a failure in your own eyes, and you only see the evidence of that. And that's exactly what I hear you saying now too – apparently that *[gesturing to the place opposite the client]* punitive side is so strong that it's filling you up completely."

3.4.3 Step 3: Have the client sit on another chair and interview the Critical Parent

In the early stages of the therapy especially, it's advisable to have your client first express these punitive perspectives in a chair that has been specially designated to represent the Critical Parent. In this way, that chair is 'charged' with those punitive messages. When your client sits in the Critical Parent chair, the aim is not for the client to speak from and for the punitive side, but for the therapist to speak against the Critical Parent, as if it were another person. By systematically linking the punitive messages to the same spot and chair in the room in the initial phase, you can refer back to that spot or chair later in the therapy without your client having to sit there anymore. In this way, you work towards your client learning to distance themselves from the Critical Parent.

> ### Placing the Critical Parent – Nicky
>
> **>>Therapist:** "If that punitive side is so active, let's literally give it a place in this room and hear what it has to say. For this to happen, I'd like to ask if you can sit on this chair *[therapist pulls up a chair to about the place where the parent mode was located just now, and the client sits there]*. Now be that critical voice, that punitive side. And I want you to look at Nicky *[pointing to the original chair]* from that perspective. What do you have to say about her?"

When doing this, you can also look at the original, empty chair of the Vulnerable Child to draw your client's attention more inward to their criticism of themselves. Many clients have no difficulty coming up with a long list of self-criticisms. You do want to know what the Critical Parent has to say, but you don't want to let the valuable time of the therapy session be filled with the very criticism that now needs to be stopped. So after a few points of criticism, stop the client.

> ### Managing the Critical Parent – Nicky
>
> **>>Nicky:** "And she can only go on and on about how miserable all that would be, and because of that she totally doesn't listen to what he actually has to say, all she does is complain and…"
>
> **>>Therapist:** "Okay, okay, I'm going to interrupt you. You're doing fine, but now I'd like to ask you to come and sit on this chair here beside me."

3.4.4 Step 4: Have the client sit on the chair of the Vulnerable Child and offer care and compassion

Place a chair in the same spot where you might have previously placed the chair of the client's Vulnerable Child. Alternatively, you can ask the client to return to the original chair if that is where you wish them to connect with the Vulnerable

Child. Again, the transition from one chair to another requires clear instructions and guidance. As in the chair exercise for the Protector, the therapist can support this transition with a calm speaking tempo and tone of voice.

> ### Transitioning between chairs – Nicky
>
> **>>Therapist:** "Please come and sit on this chair next to me. But bear in mind that when you get up from that chair, I'd like you to leave the angry, critical voice behind. This *[gesturing at the chair of the Critical Parent]* is where you can express all that criticism, but when you get up from that chair, leave the punitive voice stuck to it."
>
> *[Nicky comes and sits on the chair next to the therapist.]*
>
> **>>Therapist:** *[leaning towards Nicky, talking in a soft tone and gesturing to the other, empty chair]* "When I hear the criticism coming from that corner, it's pretty harsh. It's not just the words but the tone in which they're said. It sounds a bit like *[here the therapist can imitate the sound of the Critical Parent without actually repeating the words]*. When I hear this criticism, in that tone, I do wonder to myself – how do you feel when all this is being said?"

Many clients initially respond to this question with an affirmation of the punitive messages. Answers are often variations on: "I agree." However, this is not actually an answer to your question as to how the client feels when they hear all the punitive messages. Fighting a Critical Parent is more effective when you clearly distinguish the punitive messages from the client's emotional responses to them.

> ### Distinguishing punitive messages from emotional responses – Nicky
>
> **>>Therapist:** "How do you feel when all that criticism is fired at you like that?"
>
> **>>Nicky:** "Well, that it's right, it's actually true…"
>
> **>>Therapist:** "Ah, now – I wasn't asking if you agree with those messages, but how you feel when you hear them. Do you feel better when you hear all that criticism *[here the therapist gestures with their thumb slightly up]*, the same *[thumb horizontal]* or a bit worse *[thumb slightly pointing down]*?"
>
> **>>Nicky:** "Well, it's obviously not nice or anything…"
>
> **>>Therapist:** "So you feel worse *[thumb down a bit]* when you hear those punitive messages?"
>
> **>>Nicky:** "Yes…"

3.4.5 Step 5: Fight the Critical Parent

The next step is to address the Critical Parent directly. To do this, you address the Critical Parent's empty chair. Face this chair, because your angry or stern look while addressing and fighting the Critical Parent directly might otherwise unintentionally activate tension and fears in the client. To transition from speaking compassionately with the client to addressing the Critical Parent in sterner terms, the therapist should transition to a different, more combative state of mind. Take the time to put yourself into that 'fight mode'. When doing this, it helps to recap the punitive messages and place them in the historical context in which those messages were given to the client as a small child.

> **Addressing the Critical Parent – Nicky**
>
> **>>Therapist:** *[speaking kindly to Nicky]* "When I listen to that punitive voice, I find that I don't agree with it at all. But it also occurs to me that it isn't the first time you've faced this kind of criticism. I see the photos of you as a child in front of me, and I recall that even then there was a lot of carrying on like this. When I imagine that, and I think of how it would be if someone spoke to my child that way, it makes me angry. I feel a strong urge to say *[the therapist faces the empty chair of the Critical Parent and says loudly]* Stop! Stop talking to Nicky like that! What you're saying makes no sense!"

Offer some arguments against what the Critical Parent says, and also be sure to mention some of your client's positive qualities. A child's basic emotional needs can be a rewarding source of arguments against the parent mode.

3.4.6 Step 6: Check the effect of the intervention with the Vulnerable Child and offer extra care if necessary

Having admonished the Critical Parent mode, ask the client how the Critical Parent responds to your counterarguments. If they are so strong that the first intervention is not enough, you'll have to pull out all the stops to win. The aim is for your client to have a corrective emotional experience, and not to have another experience in which the parent mode is all-powerful and invincible. Employing drama techniques when fighting the Critical Parent, such as using a louder voice, hand gestures and/or standing up to visually dominate, can help you to defeat and silence the Critical Parent.

> ### Banishing the Critical Parent – Nicky
>
> **>>Therapist:** "That's good to hear! And how does he *[gesturing to the Critical Parent's chair]* respond to what I'm saying? Is he behaving?"
>
> **>>Nicky:** "Him? No, he wouldn't let you speak to him like that and would just get angry at you."
>
> **>>Therapist:** "Oh, he's getting angrier? Then he should get out of here!"
>
> *[The therapist stands up, diagonally in front of Nicky facing the empty chair of the Critical Parent. He stands again addresses the Critical Parent clearly, in a strict voice, supported by resolute gestures.]*
>
> **>>Therapist:** "I've had it up to here with you – I won't stand by while you talk to Nicky like that! She isn't the problem, you are *[turns around to Nicky and speaks softly]* You aren't the problem, he is." *[The therapist points towards the Critical Parent and speaks in a stern voice.]*
>
> **>>Therapist:** "I want you to leave now."
>
> *[The therapist points to the door, picks up the chair, opens the door, removes the chair from the room, closes the door and sits down beside Nicky again].*
>
> **>>Therapist:** "This is a safe place for you, where there is care and support, and no place for those old critical messages that don't make any sense. How do you feel now that the Critical Parent is gone?"

Standing up and speaking to an empty chair with so much emotion can feel somewhat uncomfortable, and as a result you may be tempted to 'rush' through this part of the process. However, try to take time for this part of the intervention so your client has an opportunity to internalise the perception that you are taking care of them. With the long-term goal in mind that the client gains a new experience that offers safety and connection, hopefully you can summon the motivation to endure discomfort in the short term and not shy away from these dramatic techniques.

After arguing with and/or removing the Critical Parent, you can express understanding and compassion in relation to the emotions felt, and you can highlight to your client the effect of that compassion.

> **Making compassion explicit – Nicky**
>
> **>>Therapist:** *[softly to Nicky]* "It makes perfect sense to me that you feel worse when that critical side rages against you like that – it seems a very natural reaction to so much criticism. I'd feel worse too if those kinds of things were said about me, especially with all that anger. And it also occurs to me that this probably isn't the first time you've heard these messages, right?"
>
> *[Nicky nods.]*
>
> **>>Therapist:** "So, it's also the umpteenth time you've had this kind of judgement cast at you, which makes it all the more hurtful. How do you feel when you hear me speak like this – when you hear me say I understand how painful this must be for you, and that I think it's a natural reaction? Is that upsetting to hear?"
>
> **>>Nicky:** "No, of course that's not upsetting…"
>
> **>>Therapist:** "And how do you feel when you hear me say that there's nothing wrong with you, that you aren't the problem here but *[pointing to the door through which the Critical Parent was just thrown out of the room]* it's him out there?"
>
> **>>Nicky:** "Well, it was nice to hear of course."
>
> **>>Therapist:** "So what feeling do you get when you hear me talk like this?"
>
> **>>Nicky:** "That you understand me… it's quite nice."
>
> **>>Therapist:** "That's good to hear! And where do you feel that nice feeling in your body?"
>
> *[Nicky gestures to her chest.]*

3.4.7 Step 7: Have the client sit on the original chair (or stand with you) for summary and reflection

As with the Protector, reflection begins with a summary of the most important elements from the exercise. In that summary, you can emphasise that the Critical Parent produces a bad feeling, while compassion produces a good feeling. Also summarise the cognitive counterarguments showing that the Critical Parent's messages are not correct, and write them on the whiteboard or on a flashcard.

What if…

…the client keeps emphasising that they really are that critical person, themselves?

First, you can explain that such self-reflections are not inborn:

>>Therapist: "I have two children, but when they began to talk, they wouldn't use words like 'bad' and 'stupid' about themselves. Children are much more likely to say things like 'Look what I can do!' or 'I'm really strong/good/smart!' So it seems that something changed for you between then and now, and you began to think of yourself as not good or smart. Who or what taught you that?"

Linking these critical messages to figures from the client's past helps to externalise the assumptions, and to see them as the result of a learning process instead of inborn characteristics. For instance, the critical side can be named by saying: 'So your father is sitting there' or 'Your father and that gym teacher are sitting on that chair, together with those school bullies, and they're saying all those bad things about you again.' However, such a link is not a prerequisite for the technique; if the origins of the Critical Parent remain unclear, you can work with the generic 'That critical side of you'.

3.4.8 Step 8: Homework

Homework may involve your client repeating their arguments against the Critical Parent to make them more familiar. In the middle phase, you'll begin coaching the client to challenge the Critical Parent themselves, and regular rehearsal of those cognitive arguments now is good preparation.

The use of symbols for the Critical Parent

Fighting the Critical Parent by speaking to an empty chair requires the client to use their imagination. The use of symbols can add to the vividness of the experience, enhancing the effects of the exercise. For example, draw a silhouette of a person on a large sheet of paper and then draw in an angry face. Or ask your client to draw it. You can write any critical or punitive messages from the Critical Parent on the paper, and then put it on the Critical Parent's chair. The Critical Parent now has a face, with visible words next to it that can be fought. Fighting the Critical Parent may eventually lead to your client crumpling the paper and throwing it into a bin or the corner of the room. A variation on this is to cut a piece of fabric into the shape of a person. The advantage of using fabric is that the figure appears large and strong when it is held up, but it falls to the ground in a limp heap when released.

At first glance these may seem like excessive embellishments of the therapy, but experience has shown that it leads to clients having a more vivid and intense experience. If working with such drama techniques does not suit you or is not possible due to lack of materials or practical difficulties, another approach is to select a chair for the Critical Parent that is wonky or wobbly – a 'backache chair'.

3.5 Chairwork with the Vulnerable Child: 'charging' the chair

In the initial phase of therapy, chairwork can help raise awareness of emotional child modes that are not yet fully recognised or acknowledged by the client. For example, a chair for the Vulnerable Child can be used with a narcissistic client who denies having feelings of sadness, fear or loneliness, a chair for the Angry Child can be added for a dependent client who denies ever being angry, and a chair for the Happy Child can be used with a compulsive client who never relaxes or has any fun. Having chairs for these modes, which then become visible both to you and to the client, contributes to the awareness of those emotions – they are there and they exist, even if as yet your client barely feels them.

However, cognitive recognition of the existence of a child mode doesn't mean that the client is immediately able to connect with this emotional side of themselves. When using chairwork, you may find that your client does not notice any emotion on the child's chair – in which case, as a therapist, you can sit on the child's chair and describe what feelings of vulnerability, anger or joy you think are present. You can try to empathise as much as possible and show these emotions not only verbally, but also in your facial expressions and tone of voice. By describing lived and authentic emotional experiences in this chair, you 'charge' the chair with those emotions, so to speak. And, by having your client sit in that chair immediately after vividly lived emotions have been described there, those experiences become more accessible to your client. The step-by-step plan below can serve as a guideline during this variant of the chair technique – 'charging' the chair.

Step-by-step plan for 'charging' the chair of the Vulnerable Child
Step 1: Establish that your client has difficulty making contact with the child mode.
Step 2: Ask your client, seated in the original therapy chair, to observe.
Step 3: Sit in the child's chair yourself and 'charge' it with emotions. ■ Describe your client as a child as you have seen them in photos, or by using your imagination. ■ Describe what emotional reactions children generally have in such situations. ■ Describe how you would feel in that context yourself. ■ Describe the emotions in the present tense and as authentically as possible. ■ Describe the underlying basic needs.
Step 4: Ask your client to sit in the child's chair, and to express these emotions and needs.
Step 5: Raise emotional awareness by paying attention to the emotional, physical and cognitive components of those emotions.

3.5.1 Step 1: Establish that the client has difficulty making contact with the Vulnerable Child

Although chairwork can be a useful tool for bypassing the Protector and contacting the emotional experiences of the Vulnerable Child, for some clients that is too big a step to make, and they do not feel any different when they sit in the Vulnerable Child's chair. This can be because the Protector is still too active and/or because the client never properly learned to allow emotions and to experience them, as in obsessive-compulsive personality disorder.
In both cases, the client answers your questions about how they feel with 'I don't know, just the same' or variations on that theme. Of course, a strategy you can adopt is to ask the client to immerse themselves in the experience more, perhaps with the help of a short imagery exercise in which he or she visualises a potentially emotional situation. You can also ask your client to take out the childhood photo that they brought along in the analysis phase and have kept with them since, to connect with their emotions better. But if none of that works, the client is evidently struggling to connect with their emotional side.

3.5.2 Step 2: Ask your client, seated in the original therapy chair, to observe

Once it is established that your client cannot connect with their emotions in the Vulnerable Child's chair, ask the client to sit on the original chair. You might also consider having your client sit in your therapist's chair because, for some time now, it has been associated with greater emotional awareness.

3.5.3 Step 3: Sit in the Vulnerable Child's chair yourself and 'charge' it with emotions

Sit in the child's chair yourself and start talking about the normal emotional reactions you might expect a child to experience when confronted with abandonment, neglect or abuse. Ask if you can hold your client's childhood photo and, while looking at it, describe the context in which that child grew up. Try to imagine how the child must often have felt as well as you can. As much as possible, base your description of the child's presumed feelings on the client's unmet basic needs.

Next, describe what normal emotions are for a child in those circumstances: 'It's normal for a child to feel sad, angry or anxious in those circumstances'; 'That little boy in the photo must feel very lonely and sad because no one cares about him.' This can turn into a description of how you would feel if you were that child in those circumstances. With this, the third-person perspective ('He/she would feel lonely') changes to the first-person ('I feel lonely') and the experiences are described in the present tense. You can help your client by allowing the emotions to be as vivid and authentic as possible, in order to make the experience as real as you can. Also try to empathise with what you might actually need in the situation described and express those needs: 'I'd really like it if someone asked how I was doing… if someone was there for me.' The aim of all this is to 'charge' the chair with emotions, to be a role model for your client and to give them words to express emotions.

3.5.4 Step 4: Ask your client to sit in the Vulnerable Child's chair and express these emotions and needs

Now ask your client to sit in the child's chair, where you just expressed your emotions. Ask your client to again try to connect with their emotional side, and to repeat the words you just spoke, verbatim. Ask them to do this, in the first-person like you did ('I feel lonely'), and to express their needs. In this way, the client is 'charged' with the emotions that were just expressed in that chair, and with this you increase the chances that he or she can succeed in connecting with emotional experiences.

3.5.5 Step 5: Raise emotional awareness by paying attention to the emotional, physical and cognitive components of those emotions

Pay attention to all components of the client's emotional feelings. Where does your client feel the emotions in their body? What mental images or thoughts accompany them? Does he or she recognise these feelings? What stands out most about the experience? How could the client 'store' these feelings so they are not forgotten and lost? This explicit and extended attention helps the client to remember their emotional feelings better, and to recognise them more easily when they re-occur.

If the exercise has been successful, your client will now feel more of their underlying emotions. By offering explicit understanding and compassion, you have positively empowered your client's learning process to make more contact with that emotional pain.

3.6 Chairwork with the Angry Child

In the Angry Child mode, the client primarily experiences feelings of anger. Here, anger is not a means of protection, but an expression of the emotional pain that the client feels when perceiving injustice. The angry outbursts of some clients in Angry Child mode can be dramatic and intense, both for the client and for you. For many, the therapeutic experience they need is to express that anger, within reasonable limits, and no longer to have to suppress it as has often been necessary in the past. This 'raging out' validates the unmet basic need of self-expression. However, for some clients, self-expression is not the only relevant basic need; there is also an unmet need for realistic boundaries. Because they have not learned to respect boundaries and to tolerate frustrations, their anger can be expressed so violently and uncontrollably that it harms them, others or their relationships with those others. In such cases, a chair for the Angry Child can provide a certain boundary for that anger. In that chair your client can le out all their anger, but *only* in that chair. In this way, chairwork can represent a first step towards learning to self-regulate anger.

> ### Assigning a chair for the Angry Child – Greg
>
> *[When the therapist starts the session five minutes late, Greg is very charged from the start.]*
>
> **>>Therapist:** "You look tense…"
>
> **>>Greg:** "Of course I look tense – I'm really worked up! You just walk in late, you don't even explain why you're late, and you always do this."
>
> *[Greg starts to talk faster and more furiously, and the therapist notices that as a result he can no longer listen to Greg properly, and he is beginning to tense up himself.]*
>
> **>>Therapist:** "I'm sorry to interrupt, but I want to listen to you and hear about everything that is causing you to feel so tense. But when you talk so energetically, I find that I can't listen to you properly anymore, because I don't know where your anger will end. So I want to quickly agree something with you, to make a deal. Let's agree that in this chair *[pulls up a chair]*, you can express all the anger you have inside you, tell me everything that bothers you – and as long as you're sat in this chair, I'll be able to hear everything you tell me. But only in that chair, okay?"

Initially, this does nothing more than assign a chair as an agreed place from which the client can continue to express anger. However, by then asking the client to sit on a different chair, distance is put between the client and the anger that now remains stuck to the Angry Child's chair. A trigger for asking the client to move chairs may be that the underlying vulnerability becomes more visible and palpable once the opportunity to express anger has been taken. However, another trigger may be that, as the therapist, you simply need some respite from the relentless expression of anger.

> ### Creating distance from anger – Greg
>
> *[Sitting in the Angry Child's chair, Greg has talked about all the frustrations and injustices he has experienced. The flow of intense anger seems to have eased slightly, but it hasn't yet run dry. However, the therapist notices that he is no longer able to tolerate the anger as well as he could initially. Signs include a tendency to become closed off, and occasionally feeling somewhat irritated.]* →

> **>>Therapist:** "I'm going to interrupt you. I do want to hear what else is bothering you, but first I'd like to ask you to come and sit on this chair next to me. When you stand up, I want you to leave all that anger stuck to that chair. Where you're sitting now, you can be angry and stay angry if you need to, but only there. Now leave all that anger behind and come and sit here next to me.
>
> *[Greg moves to the chair next to the therapist.]*
>
> **>>Therapist:** *[with a quiet, reflective tone]* "Here, I'd like to ask you to take a moment with me, with the little bit of distance we now have, to look back at the anger in that other chair."

The above examples of chairwork relate to the Angry Child, and the chair technique is an effective tool for learning to self-regulate this anger. However, for many clients – such as dependent or avoidant clients – there may actually be too little anger. Earlier in this chapter, we described how chairwork can then help clients learn how to connect with that anger, and in Chapter 5 we will describe a chair technique in which the client is encouraged to express that anger.

3.7 Chairwork with the Healthy Adult

In the initial phase of therapy, the client's Healthy Adult is not yet strongly present. As a result, chairwork focuses primarily on Protectors, Critical Parents and child modes. You provide a role model for the Healthy Adult when you demonstrate how to deal with those modes, and you address the client's Healthy Adult directly when the client is sitting in the therapy chair, or at the end of a chairwork session when you both stand to look at and discuss the chairs used. In the next phase of therapy, the middle phase, chairwork is used to develop the Healthy Adult more explicitly.

3.8 Chapter summary

This chapter has described how to use chairwork with different modes in the initial phase of therapy. With a Protector, chairwork provides a means to negotiate. The client generally sits in the Protector's chair during that negotiation, and you provide plenty of reassurance and control over the process – for example by offering the option for the client to return to this chair at any time. In chairwork with a Critical Parent, the client sits in another chair while the therapist challenges the parent mode's empty chair. You do not offer the client the option to return to that chair at any time. Indeed, you can even place that empty chair outside the therapy room as a message to the client that the Critical Parent needs to be replaced with more adaptive, healthier messages.

In the initial phase, much attention is paid to child modes. For example, chairwork is used to reveal less obvious emotions underlying these modes. The therapist can even make those emotions of fear, sadness, anger or joy more visible by sitting in the child mode chair and articulating them, thereby 'charging' that chair with emotions. Chairwork for the Healthy Adult side of the client is limited in this initial phase of therapy to reflecting on the corrective emotional experiences generated by the therapist from the original therapy chair or from a standing position. The next chapter describes the use of chairwork during the middle phase of therapy – the phase in which the Healthy Adult side of the client must learn to handle the other modes independently.

Chapter 4:
The middle phase of therapy

Chapter 4: The middle phase of therapy

Chapter map	
4.1	Introduction
4.2	The Healthy Adult
4.3	What does a Healthy Adult do?
4.4	Chairwork with the Healthy Adult in the middle phase – the three steps
4.5	Chairwork with a Protector in the middle phase
4.6	Chairwork with a Critical Parent in the middle phase
4.7	Chairwork with a child mode in the middle phase
4.8	Chapter summary

4.1 Introduction

The initial phase of therapy is intended to make the client more aware of the different modes involved in generating symptoms, and to provide them with new, corrective emotional experiences. These experiences then provide a basis for the client's Healthy Adult to develop. In the middle phase, the client learns to handle the modes and their associated emotions on their own. To increase autonomy, the therapist's role changes from leading to coaching and, in this role, they provide the client with more space to develop independence. Chairwork in this phase is focused on strengthening the client's Healthy Adult and coaching it in handling the Protector, the Critical Parent and the child modes.

4.2 The Healthy Adult

To begin, clients must learn to distinguish the Healthy Adult mode from the other modes. Many clients with personality problems will never have had a good example of a Healthy Adult. For the most part, they have had to learn to survive in an environment with punitive, demanding or guilt-inducing messages. Because of this, such clients tend to define 'healthy' in terms of 'being strong and not showing emotions', or 'always being critical of yourself and never being satisfied with yourself or what you do'. This means that becoming aware of a more nuanced and adaptive Healthy Adult side is a process in itself. A first step in that process is learning to visualise the Healthy Adult.

4.2.1 Visualising the Healthy Adult

You can use an imagery exercise to teach clients how to form a mental image of the Healthy Adult and its different characteristics (modalities). Imagery exercises can create a sense of realness (Lang, 1978), and vivid images can contribute to the awareness and lived experience of the Healthy Adult mode. A step-by-step plan is given below that can serve as a guide for the exercise. These and other imagery exercises with the Healthy Adult are described in detail in the book Imagery Rescripting: Theory and Practice (Van der Wijngaart, 2021).

Step-by-step plan for learning to visualise the Healthy Adult*
Step 1: Provide a rationale for the exercise
Step 2: The therapist gives a personal example of their own Healthy Adult
Step 3: The client visualises their own Healthy Adult
Step 4: Determine the emotional, cognitive and behavioural characteristics of this mode
Step 5: Review and homework

* Adapted from *Imagery Rescripting: Theory and Practice* (Van der Wijngaart, 2021, Pavilion)

4.2.2 Step 1: Provide a rationale for the exercise

Explain to the client that you are now in the middle phase of therapy, and the first goal in this phase is for them to become more aware of their Healthy Adult. The better the client can recognise the Healthy Adult, the better they will be able to attain that state. Next, introduce the imagery exercise as a tool to determine the cognitive, emotional and behavioural characteristics of this mode.

> **Introducing the middle phase – Nicky**
>
> **>>Therapist:** "So, I've realised that this is the twenty-sixth time we've seen each other, which means we're now in the middle phase of therapy. Do you remember the plan we discussed at the beginning?"
>
> **>>Nicky:** "Are we that far already?"
>
> **>>Therapist:** "How do you feel about that – about us being in the middle phase?"
>
> **>>Nicky:** "Well... I don't know, a bit tense because that means we're already heading towards the end, and I don't feel like I'm ready for that at all yet."
>
> **>>Therapist:** "No, not yet, but it will come, I'm confident of that. I wouldn't expect you to feel ready to finish yet. But it does mean that we'll bring in more of your Healthy Adult side in this phase. In the upcoming sessions, I want to help you strengthen that side of yourself so you'll be able to do more independently and have more confidence to continue on your own soon."
>
> **>>Nicky:** "Er..."
>
> **>>Therapist:** "You've heard me mention it before, right – the 'Healthy Adult'?"
>
> **>>Nicky:** "Yes."
>
> **>>Therapist:** "And I think you understand what it refers to. But if that healthy side of you is to take over more, we need to pay more attention to it. What does the Healthy Adult side of you look like? As we did with the other sides, I also want to figure out how we can recognise the Healthy Adult side of you. Because the better you know that part of yourself, the easier it will be for you to contact it. That's what I'd like to spend some time on today, what your Healthy Adult looks like. Agreed?"
>
> **>>Nicky:** "Sure."

4.2.3 Step 2: The therapist gives a personal example of their own Healthy Adult

Next, give a personal example of what your own Healthy Adult looks like. This could be based on a difficult situation from your life, in which old patterns were activated but you managed to handle them in a healthy way. It is not essential to give a personal example, but it is preferable for two reasons. First, it illustrates that being a Healthy Adult does not mean that everything is easy and problem-free. The presence of schemas does not determine whether or not you are a Healthy Adult; far more important is how you handle those schemas and problematic situations, and by giving a personal example you outline a realistic goal for the therapy – the client learning to deal with sometimes recurring, painful situations or triggers. And second, with a personal example you provide space for emotional growth. If, as a therapist, you remain on a pedestal – as someone who never seems to suffer from feelings of fear, sadness or anger – this does not promote emotional growth and autonomy in the client, nor strengthen your relationship with them. By sharing these kinds of feelings, you become more human and, in the middle phase, offer space for clients to grow in their autonomy.

> ### Giving an example of the Healthy Adult – Nicky
>
> **>>Therapist:** "Remember, what I'm saying to you now applies just as much to me. The better I know what my Healthy Adult looks like, the better I can connect with it when I find myself in a difficult situation. In those moments, I find it helpful to close my eyes and think back to a situation where I was that Healthy Adult – where I handled a difficult situation well, and I was pleased with myself. And by visualising that situation again now, I can become that Healthy Adult again to some extent."
>
> *[Therapist closes his eyes.]*
>
> **>>Therapist:** "So, if I had to do that now, I'd close my eyes and think back, for example, to a situation earlier this week. You know I have growing children. This week, my son was up late gaming. I told him to stop, but he started arguing. Thinking back to that moment, I immediately feel the same reaction I had then – an inclination to give in, because 'it's the holidays and he's having so much fun and…'"
>
> *[Therapist opens his eyes.]*
>
> **>>Therapist:** And I recognise that reaction in myself. It's the part of me that cares for others by being kind and giving in. It isn't my Healthy Adult; I only get to that later. So, if I fast-forward a bit in that memory…"
>
> *[Therapist closes eyes again for a moment.]*
>
> **>>Therapist:** "Then I see myself standing there, calm but firm. I remember thinking, 'The reality is that he needs boundaries too'. And saying those words again now, and going back into that experience completely, I get that same feeling again, which I feel here *[therapist points to the stomach]* – a kind of calmness, balance and strength. I also notice that I sit up a bit straighter *[therapist sits up straighter]* and I feel more solid, balanced *[therapist opens his eyes]*. Do you notice that anything has changed about me, along the lines of what I'm describing?"
>
> **>>Nicky:** "Yes, you're sitting sit up straighter… and you sound different."
>
> **>>Therapist:** "Oh, how do I sound?"

>>**Nicky:** "Calmer or something… solid."

>>**Therapist:** "I can relate to that. I especially felt that I sat up straighter – you noticed that too?"

>>**Nicky:** "Yes."

>>**Therapist:** "And I also had an image of myself when I did it; I saw myself with a calmly relaxed but firm look. I don't know if that was only a feeling."

>>**Nicky:** "No, it's true, you also looked a bit different, you acted differently or something."

>>**Therapist:** "Great! And that's my Healthy Adult. He sits up straight, says things like 'The reality is…' and stays calm but firm. It's that feeling in the belly, something like balance; that's my Healthy Adult. And all those aspects – the attitude, the words, the feeling, the image of my face, and the memory itself – are actually gateways to my Healthy Adult. When I say those words, or sit up straighter and recall that memory, I'm using a key that opens the gate. So the more awareness I have of those keys, about those characteristics, the better I can use them. Does that make sense?"

>>**Nicky:** "Yes."

>>**Therapist:** "And now I'd like to work with you to get a picture of your own Healthy Adult. Just close your eyes for the next five or ten minutes and let a memory of your Healthy Adult side emerge."

[Nicky closes her eyes.]

4.2.4 Step 3: The client visualises their own Healthy Adult

You now invite your client to call up a visual image of their Healthy Adult. To do this, ask them to think back to a situation they found difficult but handled well; that they can look back on with some satisfaction or pride. During this visualisation, ask your client to reflect on the awkward part of the memory first, and to become aware of the emotions that arise. This phase of imagining focuses on awareness of pain from the past, and the emotional side that is activated. Then, ask your client to focus on the part of the memory in which they handled these emotions and the situation well. When visualising this part, explicitly mention that this is your client's Healthy Adult side in action.

Visualising the Healthy Adult – Nicky

>>**Therapist:** "Try to bring to mind a memory of a situation in which you encountered your Healthy Adult. These will mostly be memories of difficult or awkward situations that you managed to handle well – moments that you can look back on with a certain pride or satisfaction. What do you see?"

>>**Nicky:** "Well, I see myself coming into work and immediately all kinds of people coming at me with questions and problems…"

>>**Therapist:** "Great. Just pause the image for a moment so you have a chance to look around properly. What do you see now? Can you describe what you see, so I can look with you?"

>>**Nicky:** "Well, I see the corridor and people walking towards me with papers. And on their faces, I can already see problems – that they need something from me."

>>**Therapist:** "How do you feel?"

>>**Nicky:** "Tense, nervous…"

>>**Therapist:** "And where do you feel that tension in your body, that nervousness?"

>>**Nicky:** "Here…" [points to chest and gasps for breath]

>>**Therapist:** "What are you nervous about? Why are you tense?"

>>**Nicky:** "That I can't do it – that I don't know how to solve their problems."

>>**Therapist:** "That sounds like an unpleasant feeling, but take a moment to check – is it a familiar one? Have you ever had this feeling before?"

>>**Nicky:** "Yes! Always!"

>>**Therapist:** "Okay, so what you're feeling is that old nervousness, the fear of not being able to do something. Right now, you're actually feeling pain from the past – emotionally you're meeting that girl you literally used to be. But now fast-forward a little until you reach the point where you feel: 'Yes, this is why I can look back on that with pride and satisfaction.' What do you see now?"

>>**Nicky:** "Well, then I see that I tell them to come to my room in a minute and that I'll get coffee first… and then I walk to my room with my coffee and there are already a few people there, and I sit down, and we talk about what's going on."

>>**Therapist:** "Find the moment when you had that good feeling most strongly, what happens next?"

>>**Nicky:** "I sit quietly, occasionally sip my coffee and listen to a colleague worrying about something, and we think about it together. I feel calm, confident."

4.2.5 Step 4: Determine the emotional, cognitive and behavioural characteristics of this mode

Take plenty of time to make your client aware of the various characteristics of this state of mind:

- What is the good feeling that is attached to this part of the memory?
- Where does the client experience this feeling in their body?
- What posture suits this feeling best, and can the client adopt this posture now?
- What about it shows that this is their Healthy Adult side? As they ask themselves this final question, ask the client to take a mental snapshot of themselves as their Healthy Adult.

> **Experiencing the Healthy Adult – Nicky**
>
> **>>Therapist:** "Just pause the image at this point and crawl all the way into that calm, confident feeling. Where do you feel that most in your body?"
>
> **>>Nicky:** "Everywhere, especially in my head, like I can think more clearly. In my chest too, that tension is gone."
>
> **>>Therapist:** "Very good. Now make this feeling bigger, let it flow through you completely and fill you up. Find a posture that suits this feeling and sit in a way that is appropriate to it. It doesn't matter whether you've really done that or not in the past, just try it out."
>
> *[Nicky shifts position somewhat and then sits back a bit more.]*
>
> **>>Therapist:** "Take some time to become aware of this feeling, this attitude, and remember that you're now feeling your Healthy Adult. This is the captain of your ship. If you were to take a mental picture of yourself right now, what would you see?"
>
> **>>Nicky:** "Someone who is confident..."
>
> **>>Therapist:** "And what shows you that? Do you mostly see it on your face? Or in your posture?"
>
> **>>Nicky:** "Especially the face."
>
> **>>Therapist:** "Just take it all in, this look and this feeling, and appreciate that this is your Healthy Adult side. This is you, perhaps at your best, in a difficult situation that you're handling well. Feel yourself inside the skin of that Healthy Adult and be her completely."

While this is happening, the therapist pays close attention to what changes are noticeable in the client – not only in posture but also in tone of voice, rate of speech and facial expression. All these elements are points for discussion when you evaluate the exercise.

You can now ask your client to direct their attention back to the Vulnerable Child, and then to reconnect with the Healthy Adult. This switching of attention is an exercise in learning to contact the Healthy Adult, and with it you prepare the client for everyday situations when they are at risk of being overwhelmed by emotions and need to connect with their Healthy Adult in order to manage. To prevent the client becoming overwhelmed, you can use elements of chairwork. By giving the modes a different physical location within the image, you can help the client to maintain some distance from the potentially overwhelming emotions of the Vulnerable Child.

> ### Using physical spaces and attributes to assist switching between modes – Nicky
>
> **>>Therapist:** "Do you have that calm, confident feeling again?"
>
> *[Nicky nods.]*
>
> **>>Therapist:** "You're now the Healthy Adult, with that calmness and confidence. But that doesn't mean that anxious tension from a moment ago is gone completely. Perhaps you can turn your attention for a moment back to that little girl inside yourself, with her feeling of tension. Can you feel her again?"
>
> *[Nicky nods.]*
>
> **>>Therapist:** "So, now you feel that little girl again, with her tension and fear… and where do you mostly feel her, is she mostly at your left or your right? Or is she sitting on your lap?"
>
> *[Nicky seems to probe a little for where she is mostly experiencing these feelings, and then gestures to her right, immediately next to her.]*
>
> **>>Therapist:** "So, she is just to your right? Then turn your head a little bit in her direction, as if you're looking at her now…"
>
> *[Nicky turns her head slightly to the right.]*
>
> **>>Therapist:** "There she is, with all her restlessness and tension – and when you see her, you might feel that tension again. But although you feel it, and you're looking at her and maintaining contact, you aren't her – you're the Healthy Adult. And I want to ask you to turn your attention back to that now. Look away from her – she's still there, but now turn your attention back to that calm, confident feeling, which you can feel in your head and chest. Go back to sitting as she sits."
>
> *[Nicky straightens her head again and shifts position a bit.]*

4.2.6 Step 5: Review and homework

In the session review, mention that the client's memory and its many different aspects are all possible gateways to their Healthy Adult. Your client can learn to recall the image of themselves in that state, and consciously use certain characteristics to reconnect – for example by adopting the same posture, or by focusing attention on that part of the body where they felt a sense of control.

The homework for this session consists of practicing this imagery exercise, and paying specific attention to the different emotional, cognitive and behavioural characteristics of the Healthy Adult. The chair technique can work well for this, so ask your client to practice this exercise in a separate chair that they have pre-selected and assigned as the chair of their Healthy Adult.

> **Summoning the Healthy Adult – Nicky**
>
> **>>Therapist:** "You now have a picture of your Healthy Adult – that part of you that feels calm and confident. That's the side of you we want to make stronger. But of course, it's difficult to hold on to that feeling when you're overwhelmed by fear and doubt. That's why it's important to repeat this exercise at home. I'd like to ask you, when you're at home, to call up the image of the moment when you felt that calmness and confidence, and then to become aware of all the different aspects of that memory – such as where you felt that calmness in your body, and what thoughts accompanied it. Then also try to find the posture that fits with these sensations, okay?"
>
> **>>Nicky:** "Yes, alright."
>
> **>>Therapist:** "Great! And if you have some success with that, I'd like to ask if you could also take a moment to think back to those difficult episodes from your memory. Open up for a moment to the fear and uncertainty you feel in them. Then turn your attention back to the Healthy Adult, exactly as we practiced today. Practice switching back to the Healthy Adult at the moment when you feel vulnerable. For now these are still 'dry runs'; but if you practice hard, soon you'll be better at bringing in the Healthy Adult when you really are in the middle of a difficult situation."

Having completed this imagery exercise, the client will now have a picture of their own Healthy Adult and the emotional, cognitive and behavioural characteristics that accompany this state of mind. In subsequent sessions, you can teach the client to contact their Healthy Adult by practicing (in the Healthy Adult's chair) the relevant posture, and consciously directing attention to that part of the body where they feel their Healthy Adult and its associated thoughts, calmness and confidence.

The next step in the middle phase of therapy is for the client to learn how to handle difficult situations from the Healthy Adult's perspective. And the key question here is: 'What does a Healthy Adult do?'

4.3 What does a Healthy Adult do?

Some clients may ask you the question "What does a Healthy Adult actually do?" If this happens, you can point to previous therapeutic emotional experiences in the therapy. Look back on these and explain the steps you followed as a therapist to provide them. The first step in handling any problem situation is not to devise practical solutions, but to have compassion for the feelings of sadness, fear or anger that have been evoked. Explain that this compassion and understanding has a soothing effect, like salve on a burn, and this is needed to think calmly and realistically about what is going on. Only then can you make healthy choices about the best way to deal with the situation. The Healthy Adult way to approach and manage problems can be summarized in three sequential steps:

1. Compassion (for clients: *"Be kind to yourself"*). Compassion means explicitly acknowledging and understanding the emotions that are evoked by problem situations.
2. Cognitive restructuring (for clients: *"Think for a moment"*). Cognitive restructuring refers to critically evaluating the automatic assumptions of the Protectors and the Critical Parent, and then formulating more realistic alternative thoughts.
3. Behaviour modification (for clients: *"Only then, act"*). Instead of instinctively falling back on old behavioural patterns, you can now try to handle this difficult situation differently, in a way that is based on basic needs.

In the middle phase of therapy, the client will learn to internalise these three steps. There are several variations of the chair technique that can be used to practice each step separately, or all three steps in sequence. An overview of these variants is given below.

Table 4.1: Variants of the chair technique when working with the Healthy Adult
1. Compassion
■ The client sits in the therapist' chair while the therapist stands or squats beside and coaches them in expression compassion towards the Vulnerable Child, who is placed in an empty chair opposite the client.
■ The client sits in the Healthy Adult's chair, and a chair for the Vulnerable Child is placed between them and the therapist. The therapist coaches the client's Healthy Adult in expressing compassion towards the Vulnerable Child.
2. Cognitive restructuring
■ The client sits in the Healthy Adult's chair with the therapist next to them. Across from them is a chair for the Protector, and the therapist coaches the client in negotiating with the Protector.
■ The client sits in the Healthy Adult's chair with the therapist next to them. Across from them is a chair for the Critical Parent, and the therapist coaches the client in countering the Critical Parent.
3. Behaviour modification
■ The client and therapist re-enact the problem situation, in which the behavioural modifications previously discussed can be tried out. In this exercise, chairs represent the various people involved, with the client sitting in the Healthy Adult's chair.
Chair technique to address all three steps of the Healthy Adult (compassion – cognitive restructuring – behaviour modification)
■ There are three chairs for the three steps, and the therapist coaches the client in going through the sequence. This variant is described in detail below.

4.4 Chairwork with the Healthy Adult in the middle phase – the three steps

In this chairwork variant, the client can practice all three steps of the Healthy Adult. Here, instead of each chair representing a different mode, the chairs now represent the Healthy Adult sequence.

Step-by-step plan for the using chairwork to teach the three steps of the Healthy Adult
Step 1: Explore the problem situation.
Step 2: Place three chairs facing the client and explain the exercise.
Step 3: Have the client sit in the first chair: Compassion.
Step 4: Have the client sit in the second chair: Cognitive restructuring.
Step 5: Have the client sit in the third chair: Behaviour modification.
Step 6: Have the client sit in the original therapy chair and repeat the messages from the three chairs.

4.4.1 Step 1: Explore the problem situation

In this phase, the therapist and client reflect on a difficult recent situation or look ahead to a problematic situation that is expected to occur in the near future. In this exploration, make a clear distinction between the client's emotional experiences, any critical self-reflections they may feel, and their behavioural response. These various elements are used in later steps.

> **Exploring the problem situation – Nicky**
>
> **>>Therapist:** "How have you felt over the past week?"
>
> **>>Nicky:** "Well, not that great, I had quite a tough time."
>
> **>>Therapist:** "Oh? Could you tell me what was going on?"
>
> **>>Nicky:** "Sure. I had a serious conversation with a friend, and I didn't like how she was acting; she kept talking over me and correcting me. I thought: 'You don't even know the full story yet and you're already making a judgement!' Normally I'd just let it go, but this time I got angry and said: 'Fine, I'm not talking about it to you anymore!' Well, I shouldn't have done that – she got sad and angry, and she left. And now I feel guilty that she feels so bad because of me, and I'm afraid that she'll think I'm just a pain and want to break up our friendship."
>
> **>>Therapist:** "Well, that does sound like a tough situation, and one where a lot is going on. What I hear is that you didn't like being corrected all the time, and she reacted badly to that *[when mentioning the situation, the therapist points to a spot between them on the floor]*. And in that situation, you felt all kinds of things – guilt, anxiety, and fear that she's had enough of you. *[When naming the feeling, the therapist points to Nicky's stomach as the site of all the feelings.]*

> **>>Nicky:** "Yes, exactly, I just shouldn't have said that. It was stupid of me."
>
> **>>Therapist:** "Okay, so that's another aspect of what's happened here – not only do you feel bad about the situation itself, but it sounds like you're looking at what you did from a distance, and reacting in an angry and critical way – saying to yourself 'It was bad of you to say that.' *[With this, the therapist gestures to a spot diagonally above the situation, as the place from which the Critical Parent makes negative comments.]* Does that make sense at all?"
>
> **>>Nicky:** "Yes."

4.4.2 Step 2: Place three chairs facing the client and explain the exercise

Explain that this situation lends itself to practicing the three steps of the Healthy Adult. The three chairs are placed and named as the three steps of the Healthy Adult – be kind to yourself, think for a moment, and only then act – and in this way they collectively form the client's Healthy Adult.

> **Placing the chairs and explaining the exercise – Nicky**
>
> **>>Therapist:** "I'm glad you talked about what happened, and it seems like an excellent situation for us to work on here. Shall we use this situation to try to make your Healthy Adult a little stronger?"
>
> **>>Nicky:** "Yes, alright."
>
> **>>Therapist:** "Then I'll just pull up three chairs *[places them opposite Nicky]*. Why three, do you think?"
>
> **>>Nicky:** "Well, I guess those are my critical side, my Protector and my Vulnerable Child side?"
>
> **>>Therapist:** "Good answer! So far, we've always used the chairs to represent the different sides of you, but this time I want to do something different. We're going to strengthen the healthy side of you. What are the three steps the Healthy Adult must take, again?"
>
> **>>Nicky:** "Uh, was that the compassion?"

> **Therapist:** "Great, you remembered the first step! Yes, the three steps are self-compassion, thinking calmly about what's going on, and only then taking action. Those three chairs are now the three steps of your Healthy Adult. In the first one, I'll ask you to be kind to yourself and express understanding for what you felt in that difficult situation. In the second, we'll take a moment to think about whether you really are guilty of what happened. And in the third, I want us to think about the best way to move forward from that situation. Let's just practice. I know it won't be perfect – perfection doesn't exist – but practice is how we'll master it. Could you sit in the first chair now?"

4.4.3 Step 3: Have the client sit in the first chair – Compassion

Once the client is seated in the first chair, ask them to activate the Healthy Adult. This can be done via posture, by consciously directing attention to that part of the body in which the Healthy Adult can be felt and the thoughts that accompany it, and possibly also via a short imagery exercise in which the client visualises their Healthy Adult. After this activation, coach the client to express, out loud, explicit compassion and understanding towards the chair where he or she was originally seated.

> **Compassion: speaking as the Healthy Adult – Nicky**
>
> **Therapist:** "In this chair, I want you to be the Healthy Adult. Adopt that posture – the posture of the captain of your ship. Pay your attention to your shoulders, your breathing. How do you feel now?"
>
> **Nicky:** "Calm… firm."
>
> **Therapist:** "Good, now maintain contact with that feeling, just be that Healthy Adult and look back at the situation you were just talking about. There is Nicky *[gesturing to the empty, original chair]*. I think we both understand why she felt so sad and anxious in that situation, right? Could you express that out loud? 'Of course you feel so sad and alone because…'"
>
> **Nicky:** "Well… it just isn't nice to have an argument like that."
>
> **Therapist:** So 'Nobody likes arguing – it's natural that you felt bad about it.' Can you say that?"
>
> **Nicky:** "Well, nobody likes arguments, so yeah… it's natural that you felt bad."

> **Therapist:** "And I think we can clearly see that some of this connects with your past, right? If you had a criticism of someone, or a different opinion, was it welcomed when you were growing up?"
>
> **Nicky:** "No, not at all."
>
> **Therapist:** "Exactly, so maybe you can say something about that too? Something along the lines of: 'And especially with your background, growing up in a home where having your own opinion was often punished, it's natural to be shocked when she's offended by your comment'."
>
> **Nicky:** "Well, there was always drama at home if you said anything critical, and it always turned into arguments with shouting, so yeah… if you say something negative now and she's offended, you're bound to think back to that."
>
> **Therapist:** "It's natural then, that…"
>
> **Nicky:** "It's natural that you're upset, because this is what you know."
>
> **Therapist:** "It's also an old sense of hurt, from the past."
>
> **Nicky:** "Yes, it's not only a difficult situation now, but also pain from the past, yes."
>
> **Therapist:** "How does it feel to say these words of understanding out loud?"
>
> **Nicky:** "Well, fine, yes… easy, calm."
>
> **Therapist:** "Where do you feel that calmness in your body?"
>
> **Nicky:** *[points to chest]* "Here."

4.4.4 Step 4: Have the client sit in the second chair: Cognitive restructuring

In the second chair, coach the client to contradict the Critical Parent or Protector that was activated by the problem situation. Coaching can mean that the arguments against the Critical Parent or Protector are repeated, expressed more forcefully, or supported by gestures.

> **Cognitive restructuring: challenging the activated mode – Nicky**
>
> **Therapist:** "Could you sit in the second chair now?"
>
> *[Nicky takes a seat in the second chair.]*
>
> **Therapist:** "This is the chair where, as a Healthy Adult, you take a moment to reflect on everything that critical voice says about what happened. What did that voice say again?"

> **Nicky:** "Well, that I was stupid for what I said that to her, and that it's my fault she feels bad – that she's had enough of me because I'm so difficult."
>
> **Therapist:** "Exactly. And why is this not true?"
>
> **Nicky:** "I don't really know. She was genuinely upset because I said I didn't like our conversation though."
>
> **Therapist:** "Of course, you're part of the whole thing, a factor in the interaction. However, feelings of guilt should only arise when you knowingly do something that isn't allowed, or something that you know another person doesn't want. Was that the case here? Were you sure that she would react in that way, and is that why you said you didn't like the way the discussion with her was going?"
>
> **Nicky:** "No, of course not!"
>
> **Therapist:** "So, how do you feel about that comment from your critical side that she's had enough of you because you're difficult? Is that true?"
>
> **Nicky:** "No, sometimes I'm worried about that, but she does say she's happy we're friends…"
>
> **Therapist:** "So, it sounds like that voice says all kinds of things that make you feel bad, but they turn out not to be true. With that in mind, what do you want to happen to that voice?"
>
> **Nicky:** *[softly]* "For it to stop…"
>
> **Therapist:** "Could you say that out loud to the voice?"
>
> **Nicky:** *[turns to the corner where the voice was indicated]* "Stop that…"
>
> **Therapist:** "Say it again, but this time 20% louder."
>
> **Nicky:** *[with a little more force]* "Stop it!"
>
> **Therapist:** "Again, 20% louder."
>
> **Nicky:** *[now loud and forceful]* "Stop! Stop it!"
>
> **Therapist:** "Very good! How do you feel now you've said that?"
>
> **Nicky:** *[with more energy]* "Good, powerful…"

4.4.5 Step 5: Have the client sit in the third chair: Behaviour modification

In this chair, you will discuss healthy ways of dealing with this type of problematic situation. The overarching theme that should direct the conversation is the client's basic needs. It is seldom easy to validate all a client's relevant basic needs in the reality of one problem situation, but with this guiding principle you can consider the best way for your client to deal with the situation.

> **Behavioural modification: considering alternative solutions – Nicky**
>
> **>>Therapist:** "Could you please sit on the third chair now?"
>
> *[Nicky takes a seat in the third and last chair.]*
>
> **>>Therapist:** "From this chair, I want you to look at the situation in front of you, and think about how you could deal with it in a healthy way. And try to keep in mind which basic needs are most important to you. If there's one thing that's important for you to be aware of, what is it again?"
>
> **>>Nicky:** "That I'm allowed to feel okay about myself, and that I don't have to withdraw immediately if I have the idea that I've failed."
>
> **>>Therapist:** "Exactly! So, what's the best way to deal with this situation without having to withdraw into the feeling that you've failed? If you were to say to Nicky: 'What you have to do now is…', then what would you advise her to do?
>
> **>>Nicky:** "Not to withdraw, but I think she needs to start talking about it… then she can say honestly that I still didn't like the way we talked, but also maybe explain a bit more what I meant by that?"
>
> **>>Therapist:** "Fine, just say it directly then, as if you're giving her an instruction."
>
> **>>Nicky:** *[towards the original therapy chair]* "Now, what you need to do is calm down and then go and speak with her. Say you'd like to reconnect. And then say that you did mean what you said, but you also want to explain a bit more what you were trying to tell her by it."
>
> **>>Therapist:** "Good. How do you feel when you say that?"
>
> **>>Nicky:** "Yes, well – calm, firm or something."

4.4.6 Step 6: Have the client sit in the original therapy chair and repeat the messages from the three chairs

The final step is to ask the client to return to the original therapy chair. Then repeat all the steps of the three chairs while your client listens from the original chair. Repeating the healthy messages, but now from a different perspective, can strengthen and amplify the effect of the exercise.

Recap: repeating the messages of the three chairs – Nicky

>>Therapist: "Lastly, I'd like to ask you to return to your original chair for a moment."

[Nicky sits down on the original chair.]

>>Therapist: "Think back to that conversation with your friend… perhaps close your eyes for a moment so you can really be there again."

[Nicky closes her eyes.]

>>Therapist: "Do you see it in front of you again? How upset she was after you had told her what you thought? Do you feel that inner anxiety and sadness again?"

[Nicky nods.]

>>Therapist: "Good, then open your eyes again, and let what you just said from the Healthy Adult perspective sink in."

[The therapist gets up and stands behind the first chair.]

>>Therapist: "Of course you feel sad and anxious – anyone would. And with your past, where you were always told that it's a bad thing to express an opinion, it's natural that you're upset now."

[The therapist stands behind the second chair.]

>>Therapist: "And say to that critical voice: 'Stop it! You're saying all kinds of things that aren't true, and that are making me feel bad when I shouldn't, and I want you to stop it!'"

[The therapist stands behind the third chair, turns to Nicky and points to the spot in front of her on the floor, the spot that was always pointed to when talking about the situation itself.]

>>Therapist: "Now, take a moment to become calm. Then go to her and have a conversation. First, tell her that you'd like to reconnect. And then say you meant what you said, but also calmly explain a bit more about what you were trying to say. *[The therapist waits a moment to let this sink in.]* How does it feel to hear those messages?"

>>Nicky: "Yes… good… calm or something. Also kind of strong, powerful, like I could do it like that."

>>Therapist: "Where do you feel that in your body?"

[Nicky points to her chest.]

>>Therapist: "In your chest? Put your hand on the spot where you feel it. Good. And now, just go into that feeling for a moment, enjoy it."

4.5 Chairwork with a Protector in the middle phase

Chairwork with a Protector in the middle phase of therapy differs only marginally from how it is used in the initial phase. Indeed, the objective remains the same – to recognise the Protector and, through negotiation with the Protector, to make more contact with the Vulnerable Child. The steps of chairwork as described in the initial phase can therefore largely be replicated in the middle phase. However, the technique does differ in a few ways. First, in the middle phase of the therapy it is often enough for the client to sit in the Protector's chair only briefly. That mode has now been explored many times, and always in the same chair in the same spot in the room, so it is now well known and interviewing it at length is no longer necessary. However, the most important change of technique in this middle phase is that the client now negotiates with the Protector from the Healthy Adult chair.

Step-by-step plan for chairwork with a Protector in the middle phase
Step 1: Recognise the Protector
Step 2: Name the Protector
Step 3: Have the client sit in another chair and speak as the Protector
Step 4: Have the client sit in the chair of the Healthy Adult
Step 5: Coach the client in making arguments against the Protector
Step 6: Have the client sit in the original therapy chair for summary and reflection
Step 7: Homework

The client's Healthy Adult is therefore given an explicit place in chairwork during the middle phase of therapy, and it can be introduced by asking your client to sit on your chair (the chair of the therapist) and connect with the Healthy Adult. Throughout the sessions, your therapist's chair has become associated with healthy messages that deal with basic emotional needs. Sitting in your chair can therefore be an aid for your client to get in touch with their healthy side. The therapist stands or squats next to that chair, and coaches the Healthy Adult in the negotiation.

A next step might be to set up a separate chair for the client's Healthy Adult. The position of the chairs can be set up with you and the client sitting either side of the Vulnerable Child's chair. In the Healthy Adult's chair, you can first ask your client to connect with the Healthy Adult using the visualisation exercise as described earlier in this chapter. You can then coach the client, as the Healthy Adult, to stand up for the feelings and needs of the Vulnerable Child.

4.6 Chairwork with a Critical Parent in the middle phase

As with the Protector, chairwork with a Critical Parent in the middle phase of therapy does not differ much from the technique in the initial phase. The main difference is that, in this middle phase, clients learn to refute the Critical Parent's arguments themselves, as the Healthy Adult. Again, coaching the Healthy Adult can be built up in phases. Your client can sit as the Healthy Adult in your therapist's chair first, and then learn to contradict the Critical Parent from a chair of their own later.

4.7 Chairwork with a child mode in the middle phase

In the initial phase of therapy, you provided a role model for a Healthy Adult who was balanced but could also express anger in a healthy way – for example when fighting a Critical Parent. For many clients, this represents their first healthy experience of anger, as opposed to the negative learning experiences they may have encountered in their past. In the middle phase, the objective is for the client to learn to make contact with the anger that they themselves experience, and to express it in a healthy way. However, negative assumptions about anger will often still block clients from allowing such feelings, and certainly from expressing them. Examples of such assumptions are:

- Anger only produces misery.
- If I get angry, the other person will leave me.
- Anger is harmful.

Because of this, it can be necessary to formulate more realistic assumptions about anger before practicing its expression. You can arrive at more realistic ideas about anger by reflecting on the question together with the client: 'What is good about anger?' Discussing this question can lead to a list of positive aspects of expressing anger, for example:

- Anger helps you set boundaries.
- Anger also helps validate other needs e.g. expressing dissatisfaction.
- Anger gives strength and energy.
- By expressing anger, you show the other person what your feelings and opinions are, and that can foster connection.
- Anger can actually be fun; think of how we laugh at comedians getting wound up about politics or other subjects.

> ### Exploring the benefits of anger – Nicky
>
> **>>Therapist:** "We've talked about anger before, and as you know I'd like you to get better at expressing certain forms of anger."
>
> **>>Nicky:** "Yes, but I really don't understand why I should. It always annoys me when people get angry."
>
> **>>Therapist:** "I know you see all kinds of reasons why anger is a negative thing. But there are also a lot of good things about anger. Let's consider that question: 'What are the benefits of anger?'"
>
> **>>Nicky:** "I really wouldn't know…"
>
> *[Therapist stands at the flip chart, writes the question at the top 'What is good about anger?' and takes the lead in listing positive aspects of anger.]*
>
> **>>Therapist:** "Your Protector conforms to the wishes and expectations of others, but as a result you sometimes do things you'd really rather not do, right?"
>
> **>>Nicky:** "Yes…"
>
> **>>Therapist:** "Exactly. Anger helps you set boundaries, so you don't have to do things you don't want to."
>
> *[The therapist writes this down as a benefit: 'Helps set boundaries.']*

After this discussion, the session homework will be for the client to read through these arguments regularly in order to internalise them more.

4.7.1 Chairwork to stimulate anger: the 'complaining exercise'

This exercise is a playful way to become more comfortable with experiencing and expressing anger. In general, but for clients in particular, anger often has a negative meaning. This stems from negative learning experiences about anger in their childhood. The playful form of the 'complaining exercise' gives a more positive connotation to anger and its expression.

The box below describes the different steps of the exercise, which are subsequently explained in detail. These steps do not all have to be completed in one session. You can think of the plan as a form of training, in which, step-by-step, the client gains confidence in feeling and expressing anger.

Step-by-step plan for using chairwork to stimulate anger – the 'complaining exercise'
Step 1: Provide a rationale for the exercise
Step 2: Have the client sit on a separate chair for the Angry Child
Step 3: Take turns to express frustrations, irritation or anger about everyday life
Step 4: Increase awareness of the various aspects of anger
Step 5: Coach the client in learning to express anger
Step 6: Express frustrations, irritation or anger about other people
Step 7: Express frustrations, irritation or anger about the therapist or the therapy

4.7.2 Step 1: Provide a rationale for the exercise

Explain that it is not enough to think realistically about anger. Anger is a skill in which, up to now, your client has had too little practice. You will now practice this skill using the 'complaining exercise'.

> **The 'complaining exercise' – Nicky**
>
> **>>Therapist:** "We're now in the middle phase of the therapy, and I'm impressed by what you've achieved. However, anger is still difficult for you – you find it hard to express anger, is that right?"

> **>>Nicky:** "Yeah, I don't really like it."
>
> **>>Therapist:** "Although I do think you've started to think differently about anger, right? What are the benefits of anger again?"
>
> *[Some of the benefits of anger are briefly discussed to activate Nicky's Healthy Adult.]*
>
> **>>Therapist:** "Great! And don't forget that anger can also be fun!"
>
> **>>Nicky:** "Uh… well…"
>
> **>>Therapist:** "Let's make you better at expressing anger, but in a fun way. Anger doesn't have to be all heavy and unpleasant. We'll sit opposite each other, and we'll take turns saying things that have made us angry in the past week."
>
> **>>Nicky:** But I never get angry…
>
> **>>Therapist:** Well, you're a human, so you will experience some form of anger, but if 'anger' sounds too strong for you, let's say it's more of a feeling 'of not really liking that…' I'll start.

4.7.3 Step 2: Have the client sit on a separate chair for the Angry Child

Place two chairs facing each other, and explain that they represent the angry sides of each of you. On those chairs, you can practice expressing anger, and your client can become more skilled at doing so. You each sit on a chair. Then explain the process: you'll take turns to mention something that has recently irritated you, or that you've simply been angry about. It is a good idea at this point to briefly recall the realistic thoughts about anger by asking the question again: 'What is good about anger?'

4.7.4 Step 3: Take turns to express frustrations, irritation or anger about daily life

As the therapist, kick off the exercise by mentioning something that annoyed or frustrated you. This is intended to be a fun exercise so think of small, practical and recognisable examples, such as being woken by an alarm when you would have liked to sleep longer. Then ask your client to come up with a similar example. By switching back and forth between you quickly, you avoid getting into specifics and opening up space for the anxious thoughts that can inhibit expressing anger. This exercise is not intended to work through any one situation completely; just to make it easier to express frustrations and forms of anger.

> **Taking turns to express disagreement – Nicky**
>
> **>>Therapist:** "I woke up to the alarm early this morning, and I really didn't like it. I had a real feeling of 'Ugh!' Okay, now your turn!"
>
> **>>Nicky:** "Yes, same here. I really felt like 'noooo…' this morning."

4.7.5 Step 4: Increase awareness of the various aspects of anger

Aside from learning to express anger literally, this exercise is also meant to assist your client in becoming more aware of anger in all its different forms. After your client has given a few examples of anger from their daily life, ask them about different aspects of the experience – 'Where do you feel that anger in your body? Can you describe the feeling?'"

> **Increasing awareness of anger – Nicky**
>
> **>>Therapist:** "I can see you furrowing your brow. What else did you feel along with that feeling of 'not really liking that…'?"
>
> **>>Nicky:** "Well… it feels heavy, maybe also exhausting?"
>
> **>>Therapist:** "Yes, I know that feeling; I had it the other day when I got stuck in traffic. I thought 'Nooooo!' and felt really heavy and tired, and I also had some kind of tension in my hands."
>
> *[The therapist briefly clenches his fists].*

4.7.6 Step 5: Coach the client in learning to express anger

The expression of anger will still be somewhat inhibited at this stage of the exercise. For example, the client may express anger in a soft tone, or there may still be a discrepancy between the content of the words and the way they are spoken. Coaching the client often literally means encouraging them to repeat the anger and to express it more loudly or with more conviction. For example, you can ask your client to express the anger more forcefully: 'Can you say it again, but this time 20% louder?'

4.7.7 Step 6: Express frustrations, irritation or anger about other people

For clients who are inhibited in expressing anger, it is often difficult enough to express irritations about events, things or facts. However, it is far more difficult for them to express themselves in a negative way about other people. Tackling this is therefore a necessary next step in the exercise. There may only be room for it after you have done the exercise several times, spread over several sessions. Ultimately, however, the aim is for the client to express irritations about others – a boss who was critical, a neighbour who made too much noise, or a family member with annoying habits.

In the same way as before, you practice expressing anger playfully and become aware of all the emotional and physical aspects involved. In this part of the exercise, too, you actively coach the client to express their anger even more clearly, even more loudly, and with even more conviction. When doing this, it is often important to emphasise the safety of the exercise. 'No one can hear you here except me. This is a safe place – what is said here stays between us in this room.'

4.7.8 Step 7: Express frustrations, irritation or anger about the therapist or the therapy

It is often tempting to skip or avoid the last step of the exercise, as nobody likes to be confronted by dissatisfaction with their own work or actions! However, it is an important step in the client's learning journey. Your client will almost certainly find it very difficult to confront someone directly with their anger – and it is important for them to practice doing so. Here, chairwork can provide an opportunity to regulate any tension that may arise. For example, if the tension gets too high, the client can sit back in the original therapy chair for a moment and continue only when they are ready to do so.

4.8 Chapter summary

In the middle phase of therapy, the objective is for the client to develop their Healthy Adult side and to learn to handle difficult situations and the modes activated within them in more healthy ways. We have described how to help the client gain a better understanding of the Healthy Adult via a visualisation exercise based on a memory in which the client was in this mode. Three sequential steps were described that the client must learn to take. The first is to be understanding and compassionate for the emotional, cognitive and behavioural responses activated; in their past, the client did not learn to react to difficult situations in any other way. Second, in the relative calm that this compassion brings about, realistic reflection on the problem situation can take place. And third, new and healthier behavioural responses can be chosen. A variant of chairwork can help clients to internalise this sequence, with the chairs representing not separate modes but the three steps of the Healthy Adult. Chairwork can also be used to practice learning to express natural, angry feelings.

The next chapter explores the use of chairwork in the final phase of therapy, when the Healthy Adult is strengthened further so that the client can handle challenging situations and feelings independently.

Chapter 5:
The final phase of therapy

Chapter 5: The final phase of therapy

Chapter map	
5.1	Introduction
5.2	Chairwork with a Protector in the final phase
5.3	Chairwork with a Critical Parent in the final phase
5.4	Chairwork with the Vulnerable Child in the final phase
5.5	Chairwork with the Healthy Adult in the final phase
5.6	Chapter summary

5.1 Introduction

In the middle phase of therapy, you visualised and coached your client's Healthy Adult to handle difficult situations and the different modes. Once therapy concludes, your client will need to do this independently. The final phase therefore focuses on preparing the client for life after therapy, when you will no longer be there to provide active assistance or support. In this phase, you aim to strengthen your client's Healthy Adult using a range of variants of chairwork. Your role now changes, from coaching the client through their early attempts at implementing schema therapy methods to encouraging the independent use of skills they have already been taught. As you allow more room for autonomy and independence, it is inevitable that you will also begin to find yourself on the sidelines; you do still have a role to play, but the client must increasingly put learning into practice.

Table 5.1: Variants of chairwork in the final phase	
Chairwork with a Protector	The therapist plays the Protector, and the client is challenged during the negotiation.
Chairwork with a Critical Parent	The therapist plays the Critical Parent, and the client plays the Healthy Adult. The client writes and reads out a (farewell) letter to the Critical Parent.

| Chairwork with the Vulnerable Child | The client writes and reads out a warm letter to the Vulnerable Child. |
| Chairwork with the Healthy Adult | The client completes the three sequential steps of the Healthy Adult independently and successfully. |

5.2 Chairwork with a Protector in the final phase

In the middle phase of therapy, you coached the client to negotiate with their Protector/s, and in the course of this you actively made the case for greater contact with the feelings and needs of the Vulnerable Child. Once the therapy is complete, your client will continue to face problematic situations that activate one or more Protectors. In the final phase, therefore, you will encourage the client to formulate and make the arguments against these Protectors independently.

Early in the final phase, it will still occasionally be necessary for you as the therapist to actively make suggestions to support your client in their negotiation. However, your main focus is to help your client build as strong a Healthy Adult as possible. One way to stimulate this is to sit in the Protector's chair as the therapist, and have your client negotiate from the chair of the Healthy Adult. This approach is described below. You may see some similarities with the courtroom method described in Chapter 7; however the courtroom method is a more elaborate roleplay where the therapist plays the prosecutor, the client plays the defence lawyer, and then the client passes a verdict as the judge.

Step-by-step plan for chairwork with a Protector in the final phase of therapy
Step 1: Identify a problem situation that is likely to occur in the future
Step 2: Explain the exercise and assign roles
Step 3: The client sits in the chair of the Healthy Adult
Step 4: The therapist sits in the Protector's chair and speaks as the Protector
Step 5: The client provides arguments as to why the Protector is wrong
Step 6: Review and homework

5.2.1 Step 1: Identify a problem situation that is likely to occur in the future

In the course of a client's therapy, the typical, recurring beliefs of a specific Protector will become clear. Problematic situations in the future may reactivate this Protector, and therefore those beliefs. To prepare for this, you can use chairwork to have your client practise counterarguments against the Protector. You can also do this exercise without anticipating a specific problem situation, in which case the exercise only focuses on the Protector's general beliefs (or rules).

> **Illustrative rationale for the exercise - Nicky**
>
> **>>Therapist:** "We don't know what will happen in the future, but we can be sure that your Pleaser will be activated again in certain circumstances. She's bound to see reasons why it's better to close yourself off and not talk about your feelings. So let's use this time to prepare. We'll explore what your Healthy Adult can use against the Protector's arguments, whatever the specific situation."

In the analysis phase, you established that there are specific situations that can activate your client's Protector. Examples of such situations might include receiving criticism, expressing anger, setting a boundary and so on. You can use chairwork to prepare your client for these specific moments.

> **Introducing the aims of the exercise – Nicky**
>
> **>>Therapist:** "We have another ten sessions to go. I suggest that we use them to prepare you for the difficult moments you're bound to encounter in the future."
>
> **>>Nicky:** "Yes, alright."
>
> **>>Therapist:** "What's a situation that you're fairly sure will happen again? A situation that you find difficult, in which you tend to conform to the wishes of others?"
>
> **>>Nicky:** "Well, there are a lot... but I think mostly situations when people say something I don't agree with, and then I don't dare to speak up."
>
> **>>Therapist:** "Yes, you do have trouble with that kind of situation. And I think it will be good for us to use these sessions to prepare you for those moments, for saying you disagree with something."

Chapter 5: The final phase of therapy

5.2.2 Step 2: Explain the exercise and assign roles

Chairwork should now be familiar enough to your client that little explanation is needed. However, you do need to explain that you will now play the role of the Protector, and the reasons why. When you provide the rationale, explain that you want to practice for precisely those moments where the Protector will be very convincing. It is by rehearsing those challenging moments now that your client can prepare for future situations in which they will have to handle their Protector independently.

> **Explaining the exercise and assigning roles – Nicky**
>
> **>>Therapist:** "Let's use the chairs again, but in a slightly different way this time."
>
> **>>Nicky:** "Oh?"
>
> **>>Therapist:** "It's likely that there will still be many occasions when your Pleaser will take over. And in those situations, because the Pleaser is in charge, it's likely that you'll truly believe that it's better to withdraw. Let's prepare for those situations now by having me play your Pleaser."
>
> **>>Nicky:** "Oh?"
>
> **>>Therapist:** "Yes. I'll play the Pleaser and I'd like you, from the Healthy Adult's chair, to contradict all the arguments that I'll make. But don't worry, I'll help you out if it's difficult. You don't have to do it all on your own yet – we're just practicing how you'll do it by yourself in the future."

5.2.3 Step 3: The client sits in the chair of the Healthy Adult

Ask the client to take a seat in the chair of the Healthy Adult and take a moment to activate that side – for example by doing a brief visualisation as described in the previous chapter. If the Healthy Adult's chair is the original therapy chair, then of course you can have the client sit there. Either way, it is important that your client consciously tries to enter the role of the Healthy Adult.

> **Connecting with the Healthy Adult – Nicky**
>
> **>>Therapist:** "In a moment I'll sit in your Pleaser's chair [*pointing to the spot next to Nicky*]. Your task in this exercise is to correct the Pleaser using your Healthy Adult. So, as a Healthy Adult, you'll have to come up with arguments as to why it isn't good to adapt to the needs of others."
>
> **>>Nicky:** "Alright."

> **>>Therapist:** "To come up with those arguments, you're going to need to connect with that calm, confident side of yourself. You have a number of gateways to help you do that consciously – your memory, your posture, and focusing your attention on that place in your body where you find that confident feeling. Just do what you need to do to become the Healthy Adult."
>
> *[Nicky closes her eyes.]*
>
> **>>Therapist:** "Can you tell me what you see now?"
>
> **>>Nicky:** "I see my workplace again. I've just arrived, and I stay calm even though there are a few people immediately coming at me with questions."

5.2.4 Step 4: The therapist sits in the Protector's chair and speaks as the Protector

As the therapist, you then sit in the chair of the Protector. Try to imagine yourself in that role as much as possible. You can describe what you're doing out loud, so your client is taken along in your transition from the therapist to the role of Protector. Once in that role, you can begin the dialogue with a typical statement from the Protector that you are familiar with from previous sessions.

> **The therapist becomes the Protector – Nicky**
>
> **>>Therapist:** "Good, so now I'm your Pleaser in this chair. This is the side of you that tries to conform and keep others happy, to avoid them being angry or disappointed. She has been there a long time, and she's mostly doing her best to protect you against further pain. So in the role of the Pleaser, I mostly believe that I'm helping you by being aware of what can go wrong if I don't do what others want. So perhaps I'll say, 'I might want something different, but it's better just to adjust to what the others want because otherwise they might be disappointed in me'."

5.2.5 Step 5: The client provides arguments as to why the Protector is wrong

The client is now given the opportunity to formulate arguments as to why the Protector is wrong. At the beginning of the final phase, it may often still be necessary for you to provide coaching and make suggestions as to what your client might say to the Protector.

> ### Arguing against the Protector – Nicky
>
> **>>Nicky:** "Yes, they really could be disappointed if I explain that I want something else…"
>
> *[The therapist leans to the side for a moment, as if briefly stepping out of the Protector's role.]*
>
> **>>Therapist:** "Aha, but now it's as if you're sitting in this chair, being the Pleaser. Your job now is to resist that Pleaser. Remember when we talked about how conforming to the wishes of others might keep the peace in the short term, but cause you problems in the longer term?"
>
> **>>Nicky:** "Yes, I'll be unhappy in the long run if I can never do what I want for myself – but it's hard for me to say that!"
>
> **>>Therapist:** *[leaning to the side again]* "I get that, and it seems to me that it's especially hard for you because you've only just learned to speak up. That's why we're practicing this now, so you can get better at it. Can you say out loud to me, in my role as the Pleaser, that you'll be unhappy in the long run if you just let me conform all the time?"
>
> **>>Nicky:** "Well, okay then… *[addressing the Pleaser]* …I know you're trying to stay friends with everyone, but doing that isn't making me happy."
>
> **>>Therapist:** *[gently prompting]* "What I need is…"
>
> **>>Nicky:** "What I need is to also do some things for myself – things that are important to me."
>
> **>>Therapist:** "Very good!"

You should begin gently, making statements and arguments from the Protector's chair that are relatively easy to cope with and refute. Towards the end of the final phase, however, it will become increasingly important to challenge your client by having them face, resist and challenge the Protector more and more strongly. Build up to this gradually as your client gains confidence.

> ### Coaching the client to challenge the Protector – Nicky
>
> *[The therapist continues to act the role of Nicky's Protector, the Pleaser.]*
>
> **>>Therapist:** "Yes, it will be nice to do what you want for yourself for a while – but you don't want to end up alone, do you? And people just don't like it when you impose what you want."
>
> **>>Nicky:** "Yes, that's true…"

> *[The therapist leans sideways and gently prompts.]*
>
> **>>Therapist** "Why is what the Pleaser is saying now wrong?"
>
> **>>Nicky:** "I don't know…"
>
> **>>Therapist:** *[leaning]* "Take your time – this isn't an easy thing."
>
> **>>Nicky:** "Well, it's not like I'd never go along…"
>
> **>>Therapist:** "So…?"
>
> **>>Nicky:** *[to Protector]* "Well, that's not true; I'm not saying I never want to go along, just that I want to do something for myself once in a while!"
>
> **>>Therapist:** *[as Protector]* "Yes, but you know how important this is for them; they've emphasised that they really want you to come along. Do you really have to do your own thing right now?"
>
> **>>Nicky:** "Pfff…"
>
> **>>Therapist:** *[leaning]* "I know this isn't easy, but I think that's how it goes in your head in moments like this, right?"
>
> **>>Nicky:** "Yes, well a bit, yes…"
>
> **>>Therapist:** *[leaning]* "Think about it for a moment, but try hard to refute it this time. Otherwise the Pleaser will take off with you next time this kind of situation arises."

5.2.6 Step 6: Review and homework

After the arguments have been exchanged, complete the exercise and return to your original chair as the therapist. During the exercise, your client has independently given counterarguments against the Protector. This is an important exercise for helping them learn how to generate and recall these counterarguments in real life situations. The exercise may also provide corrective emotional experiences, such as a sense of competence or self-acceptance. During the review, you and your client should look back on the exercise and evaluate what experience was gained. A useful homework task is to have the client write down any meaningful arguments and experiences you have explored in this session, and to repeat them in the period between sessions.

5.3 Chairwork with a Critical Parent in the final phase

The six steps of chairwork with a Protector in the final phase of therapy described in the previous section can also be used when working with a Critical Parent, so the exercise is very similar. In the same way as with a Protector, the final phase of treatment focuses on having your client practice applying counterarguments to the Critical Parent more independently. And just as with a Protector, you, the therapist, will play the role of the Critical Parent, holding their views and beliefs, and the client will take on the role of the Healthy Adult. There is also a similarity in the gradual build-up of the exercise; you will be relatively gentle in your role at first, but then become increasingly severe as the phase progresses. When working with the Critical Parent, it is recommended that you prepare for the exercise by listing all the counterarguments before you actually begin practicing. Your client will often still find it difficult to remember rational counterarguments during the exercise itself. Also, when playing the Critical Parent, it is important that you should emphasise strongly that you are playing a role, and that this is not your own opinion.

5.3.1 Letter to the Critical Parent

In the initial phase of therapy, as the therapist you took the lead in caring for the Vulnerable Child and the Critical Parent's assertions (e.g., 'Nicky is bad') were combated with opposing and healthier counterarguments (e.g. 'She is not bad, she is a valuable person with very nice qualities'). However, these assertions are not necessarily realistic. For instance, humans are complex, and no one is just 'good' or 'bad'. This applies to both the client and the attachment figures who formed the Critical Parent. If your client continues to see things in 'black and white' like this, they will remain vulnerable to disappointment and confusion in a life that is filled with shades of grey. As a result, it is important to work on more nuanced and therefore realistic images of oneself and others in the final phase.

The integration of both positive and negative aspects into one's own self-image and the image of significant others can be confusing for your client. For example, perhaps they have just been enabled to get angry at their father about all the criticism he gave them in the past – but at the same time, that critical and neglectful father may have turned out to be a wonderful grandfather to his grandchildren. It can also be confusing that self-criticism does not necessarily come from the Critical Parent; it can also be an aspect of the Healthy Adult. Forming this kind of nuanced, more realistic image takes time and practice. Methods and techniques from cognitive therapy, such as multidimensional assessment, can contribute to the process, and chairwork then enables this 'theoretical knowledge on paper' to be experienced more tangibly.

One approach for putting cognitive and chairwork techniques together in this way is a chair exercise in which the client develops more nuanced and realistic ideas about important attachment figures by reading out a letter they have written to the Critical Parent. In this letter, the client writes about how damaging the other person's messages were. But they can also acknowledge and appreciate positive aspects of the person, if there were any. The letter ends with the message that the Healthy Adult is now strong enough to stand up to the messages of the Critical Parent. If applicable and realistic, the need to establish a different, healthier form of contact with the parent can also be expressed.

Your client should read out this letter from the chair of the Healthy Adult, and as they read, they should face an empty chair that represents the significant other. That representation can be further supported by placing a photo or other more abstract symbol of the other person on the seat.

Reading a letter to the Critical Parent – Nicky

>>**Therapist:** "I read the letter to your father that you sent me. I thought it was really good!"

>>**Nicky:** "Thank you. It was very difficult for me, but I managed."

>>**Therapist:** "You managed really well! Did you read back through it after it was done?"

>>**Nicky:** "No not really. I was just glad it was finished."

>>**Therapist:** "That's okay. But I do think the messages you've put to paper are very important and valuable. And I really want you to internalise those messages as much as possible. That's why I'd like to do an exercise with you today."

>>**Nicky:** "What kind of exercise?"

>>**Therapist:** "I'll pull up another chair [slides an extra chair opposite the client] and I'd like to ask you to imagine your father sitting there. Just close your eyes for a moment."

[Nicky closes her eyes.]

Chapter 5: The final phase of therapy

>>**Therapist:** "Now bring up an image of your father… do you see him?"

[Nicky nods.]

>>**Therapist:** "Take a moment to have a good look at him… his face… how he's sitting there in the chair opposite you. Okay, open your eyes."

[Nicky opens her eyes.]

>>**Therapist:** "Now take out your letter. Could you read it out loud to him?"

[Nicky takes the letter and starts reading aloud.]

>>**Nicky:** "Dad, I want to tell you that the things you used to say to me hurt a lot. You often said that I was stupid, and that I couldn't do anything right. And you always said that angrily, without adding anything nice or apologising later. It made me feel like a failure, as if it would have been better if I hadn't been there. That was because of you – you should never have said those things, and I really blame you for that. I know you may not have even realised this, but you should have. It was your responsibility as a parent. You were not a good parent to me. I find that hard to say, but it's true."

[Nicky pauses and takes a deep breath.]

>>**Nicky:** "But just because you weren't a good father to me, that doesn't make you a bad person. You aren't, and you're a great grandfather to my daughter. I wish I'd known you like that as a father. But I think you never learned to deal with feelings, or to always be kind to children even when you're frustrated or tired. I know there was never any discussion in your home when you were growing up, so I can understand that being a father must have been difficult for you. But you should have learned that when you had small children. You didn't, and so I'm left with wounds that I'm still trying to heal. But I'll be able to do it, Dad. I have help now, and I feel I'm getting stronger and stronger."

[Nicky pauses and takes another breath.]

>>**Nicky:** "When I'm strong enough, I'll be able to enjoy life a bit more. Then, I'd like to get back in touch with you. With all the anger and sadness, but also the love that I feel, I want to try to find a way forward. Maybe I'll let you read this letter then, because it would help if you understood better how you hurt me. But whether you understand or not, I'm doing this first and foremost for myself. I want to keep reminding myself that the pain, the sadness and the fear I felt were not my fault – they were because you didn't take good care of me. And with that, I want to free myself from that voice that still constantly tells me that I'm stupid, that I can't do anything right. When I'm freer from that, I want to reconnect with you, and to get to know you as a dad like you are as a grandpa – attentive and loving."

[Nicky sits back and exhales.]

> **Nicky:** "That was it."
>
> **Therapist:** "How do you feel now?"
>
> **Nicky:** "Sad… but also good. It's good to express it this way."
>
> **Therapist:** "Yes?"
>
> **Nicky:** "Yes – it's good to say out loud that he hurt me, but it's also good to say that he can be nice too… and that I missed that side of him, and I want to get to know it now if I can."
>
> **Therapist:** "Beautifully said. Very well done, Nicky."

5.4 Chairwork with the Vulnerable Child in the final phase

The technique described above in which a letter is read out loud can also be used for the Vulnerable Child. In a warm, realistic letter to the Vulnerable Child, positive and negative aspects of oneself can be integrated. The letter can again acknowledge the emotional pain that was caused in the past, and it can mention less positive sides to the client, but it can also re-emphasise the positive attributes of the Vulnerable Child. The letter is read out by the client from the chair of the Healthy Adult. When doing this, the client turns to face the chair of the Vulnerable Child, perhaps with a childhood photo on it to make that mode more visible. A variation on this technique is for the client to read the letter with a mirror in front of them; in this way, the client faces the inner child even more explicitly.

> **Reading a letter to the Vulnerable Child – Nicky**
>
> **Therapist:** "Today I want to do an exercise in which you read out the letter you wrote to Little Nicky – is that okay with you? I'll just put a chair over here…"
>
> *[The therapist places a chair opposite Nicky.]*
>
> **Therapist:** "And I want you to imagine Little Nicky sitting in this chair. That little girl you used to be, and who you still carry with you. Can you put the photo of her on that chair?"
>
> *[Nicky takes the photo out of her bag and puts it on the seat of the chair.]*

Chapter 5: The final phase of therapy

>>**Therapist:** "Just look at her for a moment and try to see her for who she is – vulnerable, sensitive, warm, but also with spirit and attitude. Do you see her?"

[Nicky nods.]

>>**Therapist:** "Well then, I'd like to ask you to read the letter to her."

[Nicky takes the letter and starts reading aloud.]

>>**Nicky:** "Dear Nicky, I know you are often still sad, and you often still feel insecure and worry that there is something wrong with you. I totally understand that you feel this way. So many times you heard Daddy tell you that you can't do anything, and that you're stupid. He never should have said that. There is nothing wrong with you. Of course, you sometimes make mistakes, and of course sometimes you do things that annoy or disturb others. After all, you're a person, and people make mistakes – they do things that other people might not like. You're sometimes very demanding, and when you're angry yes – you can be fierce. And sometimes you find it hard to learn things, so you keep making mistakes when people expect you not to. But that doesn't make you a bad person, or a stupid person. I want you to stop listening to Daddy's voice when he used to say that. We take the mistakes we make along with us through life, and they make us who we are – along with all the beautiful, fun, clever things we've done. It's like a rainbow with all the colours in it, including the dark ones. The mistakes we've made don't need to be brushed away or denied, they're part of a whole. But they shouldn't be magnified either, like Daddy did. You're a good person and a nice person, and I'm proud of who you are – with all your colours, dark and light! I love you. Love, Nicky."

[Nicky sits back, looking relieved.]

>>**Nicky:** "That was it."

>>**Therapist:** "How do you feel?"

>>**Nicky:** "A bit emotional… but okay. It's good like that."

>>**Therapist:** "Where do you feel that sensation in your body?"

[Nicky points to her chest.]

>>**Nicky:** "It does hurt a bit to dwell on things like that, but it's true what I say – I do feel that way, and that makes it a kind of calm pain."

5.5 Chairwork with the Healthy Adult in the final phase

In the middle phase of therapy, the three steps of the Healthy Adult were introduced and practiced with three separate chairs (see Chapter 4). These chairs represented the three sequential steps of the Healthy Adult – compassion, cognitive restructuring and behaviour modification. Your role as a therapist in the final phase is to help your client learn to go through these steps independently. You promote autonomy and self-responsibility – for example by asking open-ended questions like 'What is the next step?' and 'How do you want to express that understanding and compassion to yourself? Go ahead.' A second objective is to eliminate the need for separate chairs for each step, so the client can take the internalised steps from one chair. And of course, the ultimate goal of therapy is for your client to learn to manage problem situations independently, and to dispense with chairs altogether.

Step-by-step plan for the three steps of the Healthy Adult integrated in a single chair
Step 1: Describe a future problem situation in a separate chair
Step 2: Connect with the Healthy Adult in the original therapy chair
Step 3: The client goes through the three steps from the perspective of the Healthy Adult
Step 4: Review and homework

5.5.1 Step 1: Describe a future problem situation in a separate chair

In the initial phase of therapy, experiences from the client's past were the main topic of discussion. In the middle phase, the focus shifted to current problem situations. Now, in the final phase, the client is prepared for life once the therapy has ended, and to achieve this the exercises increasingly focus on situations in the future. The client describes a problematic situation from a different chair, and talks about the automatic emotional, cognitive and behavioural reactions that such situations evoke. In this exercise, the therapy chair is that of the Healthy Adult and the separate chair does not represent another side of your client, or one of the three steps of the Healthy Adult, but the persistent symptom(s) that the client has experienced for a long time.

> ### Describing a future problem situation – Nicky
>
> **>>Therapist:** "So, we have a few more sessions to go and then your therapy will be over."
>
> **>>Nicky:** "Yes, it's gone really quickly… I don't really know if it's actually going to work."
>
> **>>Therapist:** "I can understand that you might feel apprehensive, but I think you've already learned an awful lot and we still have plenty of opportunities to prepare you for the time after therapy. So, what do you think are typical problem situations that might occur in the future?"
>
> **>>Nicky:** "Well, maybe a friend or acquaintance might say something I don't agree with – for example they might suggest doing something I don't feel like doing, or they might express an opinion that's different from mine. Those are difficult situations for me."
>
> **>>Therapist:** "Yes, I recognise that – standing up for your own opinions or needs, that has always been stressful for you, hasn't it?"
>
> **>>Nicky:** "Yes."
>
> **>>Therapist:** "Okay, then let's practice with a situation like that today, a situation that is yet to happen. A situation that we can prepare you for now. The kind of situation where a friend or acquaintance expresses an opinion you disagree with, for example."
>
> **>>Nicky:** "Good."
>
> **>>Therapist:** "Then I'd like to ask you to take a seat in this chair."
>
> *[Nicky sits on the chair that is placed directly opposite the original therapy chair.]*
>
> **>>Therapist:** "In this chair, I'd like you to step into the kind of situation where a friend expresses an opinion you disagree with. You can close your eyes for a moment to get a picture of it."
>
> *[Nicky closes her eyes.]*
>
> **>>Therapist:** "Try to make it as real as possible. What do you see now?"
>
> **>>Nicky:** "So, I see this friend who keeps interrupting me and telling me how she sees things, without asking if that makes sense to me."
>
> **>>Therapist:** "And what do you feel now?"

>>**Nicky:** "Angry… irritated… but also immediately afraid of having to do something about it. I don't want any drama. Then I think: 'Oh well, I know about the situation myself, I don't need to tell her'. And then I find I just want to talk about something else, anything else just to stop this."

5.5.2 Step 2: Connect with the Healthy Adult in the original therapy chair

The exercise continues as the client connects with the Healthy Adult.

Connecting with the Healthy Adult in the original therapy chair – Nicky

>>**Therapist:** "Now come and sit back on this chair *[pointing to the client's original therapy chair]*. This is the chair of your Healthy Adult. Take a moment to get into the feeling, the experience. You might want to recall that image, that memory in which you were that Healthy Adult."

[Nicky closes her eyes.]

>>**Therapist:** "And once you have that image, perhaps you can also adopt that posture again, and sit up a little straighter."

[Nicky sits up a little straighter.]

>>**Therapist:** "Good… and what are those words again, that are characteristic of your Healthy Adult?"

>>**Nicky:** "My needs matter, too."

>>**Therapist:** "Very good. How do you feel?"

5.5.3 Step 3: The client goes through the three steps of the Healthy Adult

Your client must now go through the three sequential steps of the Healthy Adult. In this final phase, you offer space for the client to have more autonomy, and you are less active with coaching and guidance. For example, leave a few more silent pauses for the client to sort out their thoughts, and ask questions rather than offering ready-made explanations yourself.

The client goes through the three steps of the Healthy Adult – Nicky

>>Therapist: "Okay, so now you're sitting here as a Healthy Adult. And we're looking at that problem situation which, although it hasn't happened yet, is likely to happen in the future."

[The therapist points to the empty chair where the client talked about the problem situation].

>>Therapist: "And we aren't just looking at an event or situation, but at everything associated with it – the fears, the concerns, and your tendency to conform. So – what's the first thing you should do as a Healthy Adult?"

>>Nicky: "I don't know… to say what I think?"

>>Therapist: "Taking action immediately? I'm not sure about that. Just take a moment to recall the first step of the Healthy Adult again."

>>Nicky: "Compassion?"

>>Therapist: "Great, yes! And how do you look at this with compassion? Why is it natural for you to feel so anxious in those situations?"

>>Nicky: "Because it's just scary to go against someone."

>>Therapist: "Great… and what else?"

>>Nicky: "Well, also I never learned that it was possible, to go against someone. It always led to problems – so yes, I suppose it's natural that this situation is difficult for me."

>>Therapist: "And is it true that there will always be problems when you give your own opinion?"

>>Nicky: "Well, it does feel that way…"

[The therapist looks at her questioningly.]

>>Nicky: "I know, I shouldn't immediately think just because I feel that way that it's true. No, of course it's not that having your own opinion is a bad thing in itself – I wouldn't think that of someone else. And I may well look at it differently. So I don't have to change the subject, and I can certainly say that I find what she's doing annoying, and then tell her what I think."

>>Therapist: "Try to imagine that. Just close your eyes for a moment and picture yourself giving her your opinion. Can you tell me what you see?"

5.5.4 Step 4: Review and homework

In the session review, take stock of all the meaningful experiences from the exercise. You can ask your client to write down the words of compassion, the realistic conclusions and the behavioural instructions that they came up with. During the review, pay attention to the different aspects of the experience during the exercise – did your client feel competent, balanced and confident? Where was that feeling perceptible in their body? Explicit attention to experiential aspects like these helps to strengthen the Healthy Adult. The notes the client makes in the review can also serve as a guide for homework exercises in which they regularly repeat the healthy messages they have identified.

5.6 Chapter summary

In this chapter, we have explored how to strengthen your client's Healthy Adult in preparation for life after therapy. We have considered how chairwork can allow the Healthy Adult to practice resisting against specific Protectors or a Critical Parent mode. Your role as the therapist in this phase is that of a coach on the sidelines of the playing field. You do still actively give directions, but you mainly encourage your client to apply the skills and knowledge they have learned from you on their own. We have also seen that chairwork provides the opportunity for your client, as the Healthy Adult, to express compassion, care and understanding to the Vulnerable Child. With that exercise, the client is preparing for a future in which they must take care of the emotional pain that can be activated on their own. Finally, the chapter discussed how to make the three steps of the Healthy Adult more integrated by using one chair instead of three.

No matter how well prepared you are, it cannot be taken for granted that chair exercises will go smoothly and have the desired impactely. As a therapist, there are many pitfalls to be aware of that can reduce the power and effectiveness of the technique. The next chapter describes some of the most common pitfalls and how they can be avoided.

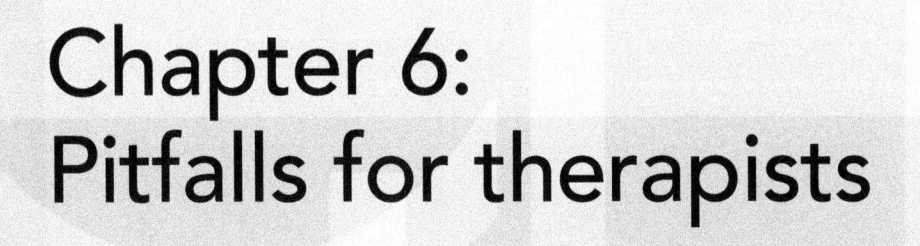

Chapter 6:
Pitfalls for therapists

Chapter 6: Pitfalls for therapists

Chapter map
6.1 Introduction
6.2 Chairwork is not used enough
6.3 Chairwork remains too technical and cognitive
6.4 The client and/or therapist becomes confused during the exercise
6.5 Chapter summary

6.1 Introduction

So far in this book, we have explored how to use chairwork in the different phases of therapy. In doing so, we have encountered several challenging situations – such as clients who do not want to engage with the exercises, clients who cannot distance themselves from the messages of the Critical Parent, and clients who find it difficult to access their feelings in the chair of the Vulnerable Child. These are sometimes very difficult situations that often stem from the very issues your client is in therapy for. For example, refusing chairwork may be the result of a narcissistic personality disorder, difficulty detaching from the Critical Parent's messages may be part of a negative self-image linked to borderline personality disorder, and difficulty in connecting with the emotions of the Vulnerable Child may be a manifestation of a client's obsessive-compulsive personality disorder.

Aside from the client's own issues as a source of challenging situations, there are also several pitfalls for therapists themselves that can sometimes make chairwork difficult. For example, a significant proportion of therapists report unpleasant experiences in their childhood that, while helping them to empathise with clients' suffering, also make them vulnerable to activation of their own schemas and coping styles (Barnett *et al*, 2007). Among therapists, 'Self-sacrifice' and 'Unrelenting standards' are the most common schemas (Simpson *et al*, 2018;

Kaeding *et al*, 2017). When these are activated, so too are automatic reflexes that are not always appropriate responses when providing therapy.

In this chapter, you will read about the most common pitfalls you face as a therapist when applying chairwork. The descriptions of these are based on many years of training and supervision of therapists, in addition to my own experience of getting stuck in clinical practice. We will look at how, as noted above, therapists' own schemas can contribute to problems. The three steps of the Healthy Adult are then used to help: first, we look at our actions from a position of understanding schema activation (compassion); second, realistic considerations are described that can help us deal with problem situations in a healthier way using chairwork (cognitive restructuring); and third, practical advice is given on the best ways to deal with those pitfalls and to make chairwork as effective as possible (behaviour modification). A general tip at the very outset is to identify and understand your own schemas properly with the help of a supervisor or peer group, and then to apply chairwork with that knowledge. I recommend that you try out the technique in a peer review group first.

The list of pitfalls covered in this chapter is by no means exhaustive; however, the issues described do seem to occur regularly in clinical practice. The most common of them is simply that chairwork is not used enough or at all in treatment. Despite having good intentions after training (or perhaps after reading this book), some therapists either do not use chairwork at all in sessions with clients, or only very sporadically. Another common pitfall is that chairwork remains too cognitive, consisting more of talking about experiences than of experiencing things firsthand. And finally, as we have seen, it is easy for both client and therapist to get confused while carrying out chairwork exercises.

6.2   Chairwork is not used enough

As demonstrated in Chapter 1, chairwork is an effective intervention and among the most essential techniques in schema therapy. In practice, however, it appears that many therapists apply the chair technique only sporadically. Despite their good intentions to use chairwork, they find there is so much to discuss with the client in any given session that too little time is left for the exercise at the end. In this way, postponing experiential exercises readily becomes a pattern for many therapists.

However, it is questionable whether being busy or having a full schedule is the only explanation for not getting around to chairwork exercises. Therapists commonly have two schemas that can lead to delaying or avoiding chairwork – 'Self-sacrifice' and 'Failure'.

6.2.1 The 'Self-sacrifice' schema

One possible explanation for delaying chairwork is that you don't want to put more strain on a client when they are already struggling. Research has shown that clients experience chairwork as intense and challenging (Stiegler *et al*, 2018). Knowing that your client may find the exercise intense and fatiguing, combined with their limited capacity, can lead you to postpone the exercise out of concern. You may think that in this way you are providing good care; however, there is a fair chance that your concern comes from the 'Self-sacrifice' schema, which is common among therapists.

Step 1: Compassion

Of course, it is important to consider your client's capacity. After all, if it is exceeded, survival responses may be activated, and your client will not learn anything new. Moreover, many clients have a background in which their feelings and needs have not been considered sufficiently. Taking their feelings into account now, in therapy, seems to provide precisely the corrective emotional experience they need. The fact that you are sensitive enough to pick up on clients' feelings is certainly a strength, and an ability that you should make full use of in therapy. Therefore, if you notice that a client is dreading chairwork, it is quite understandable that you might be tempted to postpone it.

Step 2: Cognitive restructuring

It is not unreasonable that some clients dread chairwork, given that it is often intense and emotional. A client may therefore not really want to do the exercise. However, what someone does or does not want is not necessarily the same as what they need. Taking care of basic emotional needs sometimes makes it necessary to do something you would rather avoid in the moment. It is important to keep in mind this difference between wanting and needing. Choosing not to do an exercise out of concern that you might strain a client may seem a caring decision in the short term, but it may have the long-term consequence that your client misses out on meaningful corrective emotional experiences. Chairwork often provides good care for the client, even if the exercise itself is intense and emotional.

Step 3: Behaviour modification

To avoid delaying chairwork unnecessarily, a first recommendation is to set an agenda for each session in which you include chairwork as a planned intervention. If possible, also discuss this in your peer supervision group, so your peers know that you plan to use chairwork and can ask you about it later. By doing this, you make a commitment to actually using the technique, reducing the chances of postponement or cancellation. You can also plan for yourself to alternate chairwork with imagery rescripting every session, and to add a cognitive intervention once every few sessions. Pre-planning will make you more alert to the possibilities that can open up when you actually do these exercises.

6.2.2 The 'Failure' schema

Another reason for delaying or avoiding chairwork may be that you are unsure of your ability to do it safely and effectively. Perhaps you are not very familiar with the technique yet, so you are afraid of making mistakes or doing it wrong. Or perhaps you are apprehensive about a client having a negative reaction, preferring to postpone the exercise until you have gained more skill. This uncertainty is normal when trying something new, and it may come from the 'Failure' schema – which like the 'Self-sacrifice' schema is common among therapists. It can be triggered not only by introducing the exercise, but also by certain parts of it. For instance, fighting the Critical Parent using chairwork requires a degree of persuasion that someone with a 'Failure' schema is less likely to possess. They then run the risk of not coming across to the client as strong enough to fight their Critical Parent, and as a result the intervention does not produce the intended corrective emotional experience. Such experiences will only increase the fear of failing next time.

Step 1: Compassion

It is understandable that doing an exercise that is new to you evokes feelings of uncertainty. If you also have a 'Failure' schema on top of that, the insecurity becomes even more intense, and it is understandable that you are then tempted to postpone or avoid the exercise to reduce that anxiety. In your past, you may have had unpleasant experiences when you made mistakes. Perhaps you were punished for them, or at least experienced a response that lacked understanding or support. It is natural that, with past experiences of this kind, you are now reluctant to do something unfamiliar that could cause your client to suffer if you make errors or things go wrong.

Step 2: Cognitive restructuring

It is important to realise that it is not a problem to make mistakes. It's almost inevitable that an exercise will not go smoothly in every aspect from beginning to end, especially if you haven't done chairwork often. With any new skill, the learning process is a matter of trial and error. On the other hand, it is also important to realise that with chairwork it is actually not that easy to do it 'wrong'. After all, the core of the process is that different sides of a client are placed on a chair. Countless variations of this are possible. It may well be that you do chairwork somewhat differently to how it is described in this book – and that this is not 'wrong' at all, but a variant that is actually very useful.

Step 3: Behaviour modification

If the fear of failure leads you to postpone chairwork or avoid it altogether, the recommendations given above under the 'Self-sacrifice' schema also apply now – plan to do the exercise in advance and discuss it with your peer supervision group. By explicitly planning chairwork and sharing your intention to use it with others, you make it less easy for yourself to postpone or avoid it. Further, make regular summaries during the exercise, and try to keep the pace gentle. This makes it easier to maintain the structure and overall aims of the exercise, reducing the chances of feeling 'stuck'.

6.3 Chairwork is too technical and cognitive

Perhaps you are a therapist who has no problem at all with chairwork, and who uses it regularly in therapy. However, despite conducting the exercise exactly as you've been taught, and as described in this book, you find that it doesn't have the desired emotional impact. You go through all the steps carefully; you spend a lot of time exploring your client's Protector, and you discuss all its pros and cons in detail. However, by the time you're ready to ask the client to make more contact with their emotions in the Vulnerable Child's chair, the session time is up. Or perhaps your client sits on the Vulnerable Child's chair but remains detached and is unable to connect with their emotions.

6.2.1 The 'Unrelenting Standards' schema

In your careful exploration, you may have identified several sides to your client. Each of those modes was described and named, and extra chairs were added to make each one visible. As a result, you found yourself with a room full of chairs, and keeping track of everything made the exercise more of an intellectual procedure than the emotional experience it should be. Or perhaps you did manage to work with all the modes, and you busily negotiated with various Protectors, fought several Critical Parents and expressed your care for the Vulnerable Child. However, you found that this was only possible by maintaining a frantic pace throughout the session, and for many clients that resulted in fewer emotional experiences and the exercise being experienced on a more rational level.

Being careful and complete are qualities that we should strive for as care providers. But a schema of 'Unrelenting Standards' can make us overshoot that. When this is activated, all information seems relevant and there is no longer a clear distinction between what is really important and what is not.

Step 1: Compassion

First, your diligence and completeness in performing the exercise are admirable. With it, you can gather a lot of information and all sides of your client are brought into the picture. The fact that it is difficult to keep this in proportion is only natural with an 'Unrelenting Standards' schema. The resulting high demands are not of your own making; they are the result of a background in which hard work and achievement were valued and encouraged. It is natural that performing this exercise, which can be complex and demanding, lends itself to that same perfectionism. Try not to be too hard on yourself if you find you've gone too far with diligence and completeness. It is healthy to be a little less than perfect, and to learn from your mistakes. Next time, you can take a slightly different approach. Applying more pressure and making even higher demands of yourself are not what you need.

Step 2: Cognitive restructuring

Striving to be meticulous when performing chairwork is healthy at its core, but the purpose of the exercise is not so much to be complete as to generate corrective emotional experiences. The care we take serves that purpose; the vividness and meaning of the exercise can be enhanced by working carefully and paying attention to different aspects of the experiences. And the more vivid and meaningful the exercise, the more it can become a corrective emotional experience. It is not realistic or necessary to cover every aspect of every mode in a single exercise. In fact, it is usually better to focus on just one relevant schema, and other schemas or important aspects of triggering situations are best addressed through conducting additional chairwork exercises in subsequent sessions.

Step 3: Behaviour modification

Within a chairwork exercise, you create an emotional experience by keeping the focus mainly on the Vulnerable Child. So, no matter which mode originally prompted the use of chairwork, have a chair for the Vulnerable Child and mention it regularly. By explicitly expressing the feelings and needs of the Vulnerable Child, you're less likely to lose sight of it during the exercise. Further, use 'feeling language' as much as possible, asking questions like, 'How does it feel when I say this?' and 'Where do you feel that in your body?' rather than, 'What do you think about what I'm saying?' Using words like 'feeling' instead of 'thinking' and 'doing' will keep both your client's and your own attention focused on your client's emotional side. Spend a lot of time on that emotional side of your client.

A corrective emotional experience is not a technical operation, but a change process within a client that needs time and attention. A therapist's actions in working with Protectors and the Critical Parent will naturally fit with how the 'Unrelenting Standards' schema would drive them to behave. As a result, there is the risk of devoting too little attention to validating the feelings and needs of the Vulnerable Child, even though it is precisely this phase of the exercise that is essential. By slowing the pace of the exercise and providing regular summaries using 'feeling language' when dealing with the Vulnerable Child, you increase the chances of the exercise actually taking on emotional meaning.

6.4 The client and/or therapist becomes confused during the exercise

Sometimes clients react very differently to how you expect during an exercise. For example, you may be fighting a client's Critical Parent and expecting them to experience this as supportive and empowering, but instead they appear increasingly insecure and withdraw looking anxious and unhappy. Or you want to explore the pros and cons of a Protector in a problem situation, but your client keeps explaining that situation in detail as if you haven't already discussed it at length. There are several possible explanations for these kinds of reactions, and one of them is that your client has lost track of their different modes. It is no longer clear to them which side the therapist is addressing or talking about. Or your client may not quite remember which side of them is sitting in a designated chair. In the resulting confusion, they will not be able to follow the exercise properly.

As the therapist, you can also get confused yourself during chairwork. As an exercise progresses, you may not be sure which exactly mode you're dealing with. Or perhaps you thought at the outset that you were dealing with a Protector, but you begin to question whether it might be more like a Critical Parent or Vulnerable Child. Or perhaps multiple sides of a client are involved in the exercise, so there are lots of chairs in the room and both you and the client become confused about which is which.

Step 1: Compassion

As annoying as it can be, it's normal for moments of confusion to arise in chairwork exercises. The technique has many different elements, possibilities and steps. Using different chairs and the transitions between them can be uncharted territory, especially if you're not yet familiar and experienced with the approach. It's natural to get confused sometimes. It's like learning a new language, where despite many lessons you might still lose track of tenses or forget a few words.

Step 2: Cognitive restructuring

To resolve confusion during an exercise or prevent it in the future, it's first important to understand what caused the confusion to arise. Your client can easily become confused if you don't give clear directions. You may have asked your client to sit on a different chair, but perhaps you weren't clear enough about which side you wanted to speak to on that chair. Or maybe you were somewhat inhibited in giving clear directions because you perceive that as 'commanding' the client; however, being clear in guiding an exercise is not the same thing as being domineering.

Confusion can also occur if instructions are not repeated, and you only explain which side is on which chair once. When clients are unfamiliar with the technique, a single instruction is often not enough for them to remember. A client may also become confused if you look at and address them directly when you are fighting the Critical Parent, instead of looking at the empty chair. After all, they have got used to you approaching them with understanding and compassion as a therapist, and now suddenly that warm, supportive person is looking at them with force and even anger. It may not be clear to your client in that moment that you are only addressing a side, not them as a person.

Step 3: Behaviour modification

Based on this analysis, there are a number of things you can do to eliminate or minimize confusion in future exercises. Be clear in your directions and tell your client clearly and simply which side you want to speak to in the designated chair. It will also help both you and your client maintain an understanding of where you're up to in the exercise if you regularly give summaries and support it with gestures when you name a specific side of the client. By always pointing to the same chair when mentioning the Critical Parent in a summary, it remains clear which mode that chair represents. This clarity is enhanced further by always placing the Critical Parent's chair in the same place in the room throughout all the sessions – and the same goes for other modes. Finally, it can help to place additional aids such as photos, mode cards, drawings or other symbols for the different sides on the chairs.

6.5 Chapter summary

In this chapter, we have considered how therapists' own schemas can be activated during chairwork. The most common schemas among therapists are 'Self-sacrifice', 'Failure' and 'Unrelenting Standards'. When these are activated, therapists can end up avoiding exercises, delivering them too intellectually, or causing confusion for the client and/or themselves. Handling these pitfalls in a healthy way is the first step to maintaining understanding and compassion for these schemas and their activation.

In fact, all these schemas also have great advantages. For instance, through the 'Self-sacrifice' schema, you offer precisely the sort of care your client has been missing; you can relate well to fear and sadness by recognising those feelings in your own schema of 'Failure'; and through your 'Unrelenting Standards' schema, you are inclined to do your utmost to provide exactly the right care to your client. However, these schemas also have a downside, which is that you can feel insecure when doing chairwork or be tempted to avoid the exercise out of concern for the client – or indeed that you want to do it too well. Your own background and development may have prevented you from learning to deal with these schemas differently and in a healthier way.

Having understanding and compassion for yourself gives you an opportunity to consider alternatives more calmly. When doing this, it is important to keep in mind that it's not really a problem to get stuck occasionally, or to find chairwork difficult. The core of the exercise is still that different sides of the client are placed on different chairs, and this physical distance allows for corrective emotional experiences. Although this can make chairwork intense, and your client may give signals that they do not want to do it, you're actually providing good care by using this technique. You can reinforce this by planning chairwork exercises in advance, in consultation with your peer supervision group. Be clear in your directions to the client, with the understanding that providing clarity as to what you want is not the same as ordering them about. During the exercise, keep the pace slow and give frequent summaries – and in those summaries, consistently point to the same spot or chair when mentioning a particular side of your client. Following these steps can help keep your own activated schemas manageable, and allow you to find your way when doing chair exercises.

Remember that many variations are possible with chairwork, meaning that an exercise does not necessarily have to follow a preconceived plan to be able to deliver a meaningful experience for your client. In the next chapter, we will explore how to a number of these variations can be used in specialist applications such as when dealing with substance use, partner relationship issues or unprocessed grief.

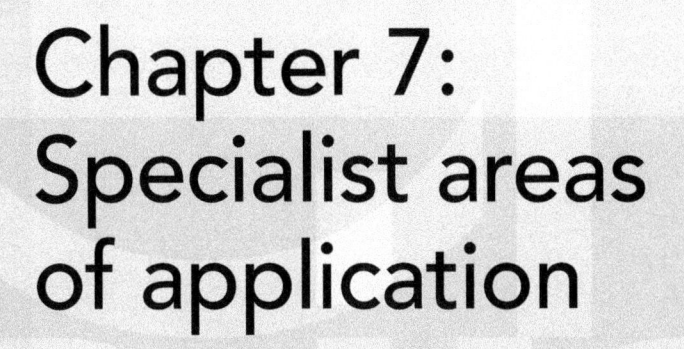

Chapter 7:
Specialist areas of application

Chapter 7: Specialist areas of application

Chapter map	
7.1	Introduction
7.2	Substance abuse
7.3	Anxiety and mood disorders
7.4	Guilt: The courtroom method
7.5	Partner and relationship problems
7.6	Group therapy
7.7	Grief and mourning
7.8	Decision making: The Future Self
7.9	Chapter summary

7.1 Introduction

This chapter describes the application of chairwork for various specific disorders and symptoms. In chairwork, chairs can be used not only to represent the different modes of a client, but also to represent different thoughts, deceased people, fictitious people, another person in the client's current life, a future version of the client, or the different options that may be available when making a decision. The effect always remains the same – placing someone or something on a chair generates not only physical distance but also emotional distance, which creates space for other perceptions, choices or options. Therefore, chairwork can be used effectively in the treatment of anxiety and mood disorders, substance use disorders, partner and relationship problems, group therapy, unresolved grief and decision making. This chapter describes these specialised areas of application.

7.2 Substance abuse

Chairwork can be used in at least two distinct ways with clients who have difficulties with alcohol or drug use. In the first approach, the chair is used to represent the substance itself or the desire to use it. In the second approach, the use of the substance is linked to a mode and the chair represents that mode. Examples of common relevant modes include Protectors, who typically use the substance to dampen emotions, and Critical Parent modes activated by the use of the substance.

7.2.1 Variant 1: The substance is placed on a chair

Clients who use substances often personify the substance – they see it as a 'friend' or an 'enemy'. This personification allows for a dialogue with the substance, in the same way as when working with modes. In this scenario, a chair can serve to represent the substance and, as the Healthy Adult, your client can enter into a dialogue with it. Depending on the meaning that the substance has, your client might wish to negotiate with it, say goodbye to it, or send it away.

> **Placing a substance on a chair – Greg**
>
> **>>Greg:** "I feel a really strong need to drink all the time. I know I shouldn't, and I know it's a real problem, but I can hardly think of anything else."
>
> **>>Therapist:** "Then I suggest we do a chair exercise. I'll put a chair over here now."
>
> *[The therapist stands and places a chair opposite Greg. Then he moves his own chair a little closer to Greg's so they are sitting together opposite the empty chair.]*
>
> **>>Therapist:** "I've added that chair so as to give alcohol and the desire that goes with it an actual place in this room. And now, I want to ask if you'd like to sit there."
>
> *[Greg sits down on the extra chair.]*
>
> **>>Therapist:** "Now close your eyes for a moment, and let your thoughts wander to drinking. Allow images to come up that fit your desire to drink… what do you see in front of you?"
>
> **>>Greg:** "If I'm honest, I see a bottle of whisky, just opened, with a glass next to it that has just been poured, half full…"
>
> **>>Therapist:** "And what do you feel?"
>
> **>>Greg:** "I'm really looking forward to it."

>>**Therapist:** "In which part of this image do you especially feel that longing?"

>>**Greg:** "When I look at the glass, the colour of the drink… it's as if the glass is saying: 'Go on, just have this one glass and then you'll stop.'"

>>**Therapist:** "Now open your eyes. I want to ask you to come and sit next to me again – but when you get up, I want you to leave the image – the whisky and the desire that goes with it – on the chair where you are now. Leave it stuck there with Super Glue." *[Greg slowly gets up and comes to sit next to the therapist on the original therapy chair.]*

>>**Therapist:** "And now look at the chair, with the image of the bottle and glass on it. Do you see it?"

>>**Greg:** "Yes."

>>**Therapist:** "And when you see it like that in front of you now, do you feel any desire?"

>>**Greg:** "Yes…"

>>**Therapist:** "We can look at it together from a distance, the drink and the desire that goes with it. And with the benefit of that distance, we can think about what you want to do with that desire. Over there's that glass saying: 'Go ahead, just one glass won't hurt.' But here, on the chair next to me, I want to ask you to be your Healthy Adult. Just take the posture that goes with that side of you *[Greg sits up a little straighter]*, and I'll also address you as the Healthy Adult for now. What do you want to do with that glass over there, that glass that says: 'Take me, one can't hurt'?"

>>**Greg:** "Well, yeah… looking at it that way from a distance, I don't want to get into that. I would want it not to be there."

>>**Therapist:** "I wonder if it helps enough just to say, 'I'd rather it wasn't there'. Maybe you can also say something more specific to that drink, to that desire. Can you tell it what your real need is, and explain that what you really need is something other than drinking?"

>>**Greg:** "Should I literally say that now, out loud?"

>>**Therapist:** "That seems a sensible plan. You're the captain of your ship, after all, and you've just realised that this desire is also on board. What course do you want the ship to take now? Do you want this desire to be able to take the helm every time?"

>>**Greg:** "No…"

>>**Therapist:** "Why not?"

>>**Greg:** "Well, because it just destroys more than I'd like."

> **Therapist:** "Okay, so tell that to the desire there on the chair."
>
> *[Greg turns to face the chair.]*
>
> **Greg:** "I know you're there and I've listened to you many times, but alcohol just isn't what I need."

7.2.2 Variant 1: The mode related to the substance use is placed on a chair

In this second variant, chairwork focuses on the client's modes that are relevant in the use of the substance. For example, the Protector might use the substance as a means to escape tensions and emotions, or using the substance may activate your client's Punitive Parent. In such situations, it is not the substance but the relevant mode that is placed on a chair.

> **Placing a mode related to substance use on a chair – Greg**
>
> **Greg:** "A friend came over and wanted us to have a drink together. I thought, 'I'll just have one or two then stop', but by the end of the night I was completely smashed. And the next day I felt terrible. All that time I hadn't drunk, and then I just relapsed big time. I'm so stupid!"
>
> **Therapist:** "When I hear that angry voice, I wonder if it isn't your Punitive Parent again."
>
> **Greg:** "Yes, I think so…"
>
> **Therapist:** "So let's work on that with a chair exercise today."
>
> **Greg:** "Yes, alright."
>
> **Therapist:** "Good, then I'll pull up a chair. Would you like to sit on it now, so you can tell me everything your critical side has to say?"
>
> *[Greg sits down on the other chair.]*
>
> **Therapist:** "On this chair, you can really go into all this criticism you're getting from your Punitive Parent. Just become that side… what do you want to say to Greg now?"
>
> *[The therapist points to the original therapy chair, and Greg turns towards it.]*
>
> **Greg:** "You're such a failure! You get offered one drink, and you can't even manage to say no and turn it down. You're just a loser!"

> **Therapist:** "Okay, okay… I'll stop you there. You're doing great, and I can really hear the anger of that critical side saying all those things. Can you sit on this chair again now? *[The therapist points to the original therapy chair]* And as you get up from your chair, I want you to leave all that anger behind, stuck to the chair."
>
> *[Greg stands up and goes to sit on the original therapy chair. The therapist leans towards Greg and speaks to him in a soft voice.]*
>
> **Therapist:** "How do you feel when you hear your Punitive Parent carrying on like that?"
>
> **Greg:** "Sad… like I'm being bullied."
>
> **Therapist:** "Exactly! He really is a bully, isn't he? I'd like to say something to him myself. Is that okay with you? I'd like to say something about what happened."
>
> *[The therapist turns to the Punitive Parent's chair and speaks in a forceful tone.]*
>
> **Therapist:** "Leave him alone! You have no right to speak to him like that! Okay, so he had a few drinks, and I won't say that's great. But the reality is that he's recovering. And moments like these are a normal part of that process. There will be other times in the future when he slips up. And then, hopefully, he'll do exactly what he's done now – pick himself up and get back on the path to recovery. You don't allow any room for important learning moments like these. You only criticise and punish."
>
> *[The therapist turns to Greg and speaks again in a soft voice.]*
>
> **Therapist:** "How do you feel when you hear me speak like this?"
>
> **Greg:** "Good, I think."

7.3 Anxiety and mood disorders

In anxiety and mood disorders, clients are often bothered by recurring thoughts that make them anxious or depressed. Clients may identify with such thoughts so fully that there is no room for alternative interpretations – they can see no other point of view. Using chairwork, such a thought can be placed on a chair in order to gain distance from it. With that distance, the credibility of the thought can be examined critically and adjusted to achieve a more realistic understanding.

Placing a thought on a chair – Greg

>>Therapist: "Okay, so when you touched the door handle, you were instantly worried about AIDS. And the fearful thought you had at that moment was "If I don't wash my hands ten times now, I'll die of AIDS". And at the time, it wasn't just a possibility – it was a certainty for you?"

>>Greg: "Yes."

>>Therapist: "The goal of therapy is for you to learn to think realistically in those situations. Now, to explore the realistic risk of AIDS infection, first of all we wrote down all the conditions that would be necessary to actually contract AIDS in such a situation."

>>Greg: "Yes…"

>>Therapist: "And one of the first of these is that a person with AIDS must have touched the same door handle just before you did. Without that, AIDS could not be on the door handle."

>>Greg: "That's right."

>>Therapist: "What I want now is for us to consider the realistic risk that there was a person with AIDS who touched the door handle right before you."

>>Greg: "100%! That is 100% certain!"

>>Therapist: "Because?"

>>Greg: "Because it's certain that someone with AIDS has been there, it just makes sense!"

>>Therapist: "Okay… again, it sounds like you're in a state where, for you, it seems absolutely certain that this kind of thing definitely happens."

>>Greg: "Yes, but that does make sense! It's a fact – there are people with AIDS!"

>>Therapist: "Okay, wait a second. I want to add a chair, because I think what happens next is important."

[The therapist stands up and pulls up an extra chair.]

>>Therapist: "I'll just put this chair next to you. Because what I notice is that when we try to look at risks in a rational way, your Compulsive Side takes over *[points to the empty chair]* and says: 'It's 100% certain that a person with AIDS touched the handle just before I did!'"

>>Greg: "But that's the reality!"

>>Therapist: "For you, exactly. As you sit there now, there seems to be no possibility other than that. And that's why I'd like to ask you to sit on the chair of the Compulsive Side now."

[Greg sits down on the other chair.]

>>Therapist: "On this chair, I want you to be that Compulsive Side fully. And as that side, you're completely convinced that the door handle is definitely infected with AIDS, right?"

[Greg nods.]

>>Therapist: "So, if I were to ask you what the realistic probability is that someone with AIDS has touched the door handle just before you did, your answer would be?"

>>Greg: "There really are people around with AIDS, and they've 100% touched the door handle."

>>Therapist: "Okay, in a moment I'd like you to sit back on that chair *[points to the original therapy chair]*, but when you do, I want you to leave that Compulsive Side behind. Leave it stuck to this chair, and then come and sit next to me."

[The therapist points again to the original therapy chair, and Greg sits down on it.]

>>Therapist: "Okay, so over there *[pointing to the chair of the Compulsive Side]*, is that Compulsive Side. He's sure the door handle has been touched by someone with AIDS. In fact, he's so sure that he doesn't even think about it anymore. But you and I *[pointing to himself and to Greg in the original therapy chair]* have decided to take some time to think about this. We want to know for sure what the risk is. So, let's take a moment and think. What are the chances that, just before you touched the door handle, someone with AIDS also did so? How many people with AIDS are there in your area?"

>>Greg: "No idea… one or two?"

>>Therapist: "So, one or two out of every hundred or so times someone has touched the door handle before you, it might have been a person with AIDS?"

>>Greg: "Yes, maybe…"

>>Therapist: "And of course, we're not done just with that. I can almost hear him *[pointing to the Compulsive Side's chair again]* already thinking: 'Yes, but that doesn't matter, because even if it's only one percent, it's a serious problem.'"

>>Greg: "Yes, exactly!"

>>Therapist: "So, we still have to examine this further."

A variation is to use two separate chairs to examine the arguments for and against a thought or belief, with the belief itself represented in a third chair. In this variant, the belief is placed on a chair in the middle of the room. Two chairs are then placed on either side of that belief, facing each other. The client articulates the arguments for and against from the corresponding chairs.

Finally, from the original therapy chair, the client can ultimately make a judgement about the credibility of the belief. This approach is somewhat like a simplified version of the courtroom method described below.

7.4 Guilt: The courtroom method

The courtroom method is mainly suitable for clients who often feel guilty as a result of perceived mistakes or shortcomings. In the courtroom method, the approach is to use roleplay to examine and change assumptions about guilt and responsibility. Beliefs around guilt will already have been examined earlier in the therapy, but if this did not lead to sufficient change, you can propose examining the feelings of guilt in a manner that would be used in a court of law.

Step-by-step plan for the courtroom method
Step 1: Determine the automatic thought or belief
Step 2: Explain the rationale for the courtroom method
Step 3: Set up the courtroom and allocate roles
Step 4: The therapist opens as prosecutor
Step 5: The client plays the role of defence lawyer
Step 6: Arguments are exchanged back and forth until exhausted
Step 7: The client sits in the judge's chair and delivers the verdict

7.4.1 Step 1: Determine the automatic thought or belief

As the therapist, once you have identified a recurring theme of guilt or excessive responsibility in what your client has told you, or in the diary forms they have brought along to the therapy session, bring this up for discussion. This will then become the 'charge' for the courtroom method.

> **Determining the automatic thought or belief – Greg**
>
> **>>Therapist:** "In the forms you brought along, I can see that there have been all kinds of situations in the past week where you become more depressed. And on all those forms, it seems there are recurring thoughts that it's your own fault that you've found yourself in that situation. Is that right?"

> **Greg:** "Yes."
>
> **Therapist:** "And this isn't the first time this has happened. In previous conversations we've also looked at how guilt is a theme in your thoughts. Am I correct in saying that?"
>
> **Greg:** "Yes, that's true."

7.4.2 Step 2: Explain the rationale for the courtroom method

The rationale for the courtroom technique is that a court of law is an institution with centuries of experience in how to best establish whether a person is guilty or not. By playing out a court hearing during the therapy session, this expertise can be put to constructive and productive use.

> **Explaining the rationale for the courtroom method – Greg**
>
> **Therapist:** "Now, it's very important that we cross-examine the extent to which the idea that you are guilty is true. We've looked at it before, but it remains a persistent theme. And that's why I think we may need to examine it in a different way today. Guilty or innocent, that's the question we'll consider. And where in society do we look to determine whether someone is guilty or innocent?"
>
> **Greg:** "A court of law?"
>
> **Therapist:** "Exactly. That means there's a lot of expertise in a court, and all kinds of protocols on the best way to determine guilt or innocence. Now, I'm not saying we need to actually go to a court. But maybe we can try to bring a court into this room, and use its methods to investigate the extent to which you're guilty or innocent. How would you like to try looking at your beliefs like that?"
>
> **Greg:** "Yes I'd like to, although I don't know exactly how it will go."

7.4.3 Step 3: Set up the courtroom and allocate roles to the participants

After the purpose of the courtroom method has been established, the therapist stands and invites the client to help set up part of the therapy room as a courtroom. Decide where the prosecutor, defence lawyer and judge will sit. When assigning roles, the client is given the role of defence lawyer as a way to actively rehearse arguments as to why the automatic fearful thoughts are unjustified.

Chapter 7: Specialist areas of application

> ### Setting up the courtroom – Greg
>
> **>>Therapist:** "So I'd like to set up this room as if it was a court. And let's take this seriously. The first question is then – who or what do we have in a court of law? Who is present at a hearing?"
>
> **>>Greg:** "Well – a lawyer, right?"
>
> **>>Therapist:** "Indeed – a lawyer. And where shall we put this lawyer? How about over there?"
>
> *[Takes an extra chair and places it to Greg's left.]*
>
> **>>Therapist:** "So, we have a lawyer sitting next to the accused, and that lawyer's job is to defend the accused as well as possible. Who else do we need?"
>
> **>>Greg:** "Uh… yeah, someone who, I don't really know what they're called, but who wants to put the blame on the accused?"
>
> **>>Therapist:** "Yes – the prosecutor, or the Public Prosecution Service. Let's just say the prosecutor. Shall we put them there?"
>
> *[Takes an extra chair and places it opposite the defence lawyer's chair.]*
>
> **>>Therapist:** "So, this is the prosecutor's chair, and their job is to present arguments that would show that the accused is guilty. And who else do we need in a court of law?"
>
> **>>Greg:** "The judge, or judges."
>
> **>>Therapist:** "Okay, and where shall we put them?"
>
> **>>Greg:** "I think they always sit at the front?"
>
> **>>Therapist:** "That's right, the defence lawyer and the prosecutor are actually talking to the judge during the hearing, so let's put the judge here."
>
> *[Places a chair diagonally opposite the prosecutor's chair and the lawyer's chair].*

A simple drawing on flipchart paper can symbolise the judge and be placed on the judge's chair. Then you sit in the prosecutor's chair, and the client in the defence lawyer's chair, and the roleplay begins.

> ### Allocating roles – Greg
>
> **>>Therapist:** "I'll take the role of the prosecutor *[sits in the prosecutor's chair]*. So, my job is to put forward arguments that prove you're guilty. Your role is that of defence lawyer, so your job is to present arguments that show the accused is not guilty. You can sit in the defence lawyer's chair now."
>
> *[Greg sits in the defence lawyer's chair]*

> **Therapist:** "In that chair, I want you to defend your client to the best of your ability. I understand that what we're doing might seem a bit strange, but in the end it's all about one important question – are you really guilty? The best way to find that out is to examine this as seriously as possible, so take a moment to get into your role. This is about whether the things that aren't going well in your life are all your fault. And it's your job as a lawyer to defend your client against that accusation. So – I'll start as the prosecutor, and actually I'll stand just there."
>
> *[The therapist stands up and turns to the judge's chair].*

7.4.4 Step 4: The therapist opens as prosecutor

In the role of the prosecutor, as the therapist, you open the courtroom exercise by stating the automatic thought as the charge. Do this as seriously as possible by standing up and turning to the imaginary judge to announce the charge.

> **The therapist opens as prosecutor – Greg**
>
> **Therapist:** "Very good, Your Honour, we are gathered here for a simple case. The defendant here had to sell his house after he lost his job, and I believe this is all his own fault. He made mistakes, as a result of which he is now in this situation, and it seems to me that he should be found guilty for that."

7.4.5 Step 5: The client plays the role of defence lawyer

Now ask the client to stand, turn to the judge and explain why the accused is not guilty and should not be convicted. By assigning the role of defence lawyer to the client, they are prompted to assess their assumptions critically. Moreover, this role-playing game makes use of a phenomenon that speaking arguments out loud gives them greater credibility than when they are only heard or read.

> **The client responds as defence lawyer – Greg**
>
> **Therapist:** "Now you. So, be the defence lawyer making arguments against this charge."
>
> **Greg:** "Well, to be honest I can't really argue with it at all."

> **Therapist:** "I get that – you're experiencing what happens all the time. You can't see any alternative explanation. But now it's your job as a lawyer to stand up for your client. You might have to work hard to do it, but make sure the arguments that refute the charge are stated. And these are the very arguments that we discussed earlier. What counterarguments did we talk about?"
>
> **Greg:** "Well, about the role of my boss… because in the end he wasn't really justified in firing me."
>
> **Therapist:** "Fine, then stand by that argument for a moment. Face the judge and make your point."
>
> *[Greg stands up somewhat hesitantly and turns to the judge's chair.]*
>
> **Greg:** "Your Honour, as the defence, I want to point out that the role of my client's boss should also be considered in this whole story. Because the reasons why he decided to fire him were, in my view, quite unjustified."

7.4.6 Step 6: Arguments are exchanged back and forth until exhausted

Take it in turns to put forth the arguments for and against the accused until all arguments have been stated. Ask your client if all the doubts or considerations have been included in the exchange.

> ### Arguments are exchanged back and forth – Greg
>
> **Therapist:** "Good. Then it's my turn as prosecutor again. Actually, at this point, I don't really know what else I can bring in. I've already put forward the idea that you're the only one responsible, that you should have known your boss would make this decision. What else makes you feel so guilty?"
>
> **Greg:** "Well, perhaps that there's always something with me. I've always had problems, and that plays into it for me. It's not just this situation – I've also had other issues over the past few years."
>
> **Therapist:** "Aha, good, then I'll bring that in. *[Turns to the judge's chair.]* Well, Your Honour, another factor in this case is that this is not the first time the accused has had problems; things like this have happened to him before, and he was to blame then too."

7.4.7 Step 7: The client sits in the judge's chair and delivers the verdict

As the therapist, you should make notes of the arguments of both the prosecutor and the defence during the roleplay. When all the arguments are exhausted, ask the client to sit on the judge's chair and go over all these arguments and counterarguments. Then, having carefully considered all these pieces of evidence, ask the client to deliver the court's verdict – guilty or not guilty.

> **The client delivers the verdict – Greg**
>
> **>>Therapist:** "This brings us to the point of conclusion. And a conclusion in a court case means the judge has reached a verdict, based on all the arguments put forward. I've written down the arguments here. Now I'd like you to play the role of the judge. Take a good look at all the notes I've made, and make sure you come to a balanced judgement – guilty or innocent."
>
> *[Greg takes a seat on the judge's chair. The therapist stands next to him and passes him the notes.]*
>
> **>>Therapist:** "So be that judge – take your time to go over the arguments I've written down again. And once you've gone through everything, pronounce your judgement."
>
> *[Greg spends time reading through and considering all the notes.]*
>
> **>>Greg:** "I've heard all the arguments from the prosecution and also from the defence, and as the judge I'm of the opinion that the defence has made important arguments in this case. Namely that the defendant in question never intentionally let it get to this point."
>
> *[All the arguments are gone through again.]*
>
> **>>Greg:** "And with that, my ruling is – that the accused is found Not Guilty!"

You can now also ask the client to repeat this verdict in the first person, so instead of "the accused is found Not Guilty because…" your client can say, "I am found Not Guilty because…".

7.5 Partner and relationship problems

Treatment for partner and relationship problems can take place in an individual setting, in which the client talks about the problems experienced in their relationship. Alternatively, both partners can be present when these issues are discussed. In either case, chairwork can be a valuable tool.

In an individual setting, chairwork can be used to allow your client to express feelings or needs without having the partner present. In this way, it can prepare the client for a real conversation with their partner that will take place in the future. An empty chair can be used for this, or the client can switch between the partner's chair and their own chair. As the therapist, you can also sit in the partner's chair to prepare for the future conversation with their partner as realistically as possible.

In partner and relationship discussions where both partners are present, chairwork first and foremost provides an opportunity for your clients to gain more insight into recurring communication problems. Partners often react to only one side of the other person and, in those moments, lose sight of the fact that their partner also has other sides. Chairwork can help to make those different sides more visible and conspicuous. Chairs are used to set up two different mode models in the room. There are several ways in which those mode models and their interactions can be constructed. A general guideline is to do this in small sections, and to alternate attention between the two partners. This avoids either one of the partners experiencing too much or too little attention.

Step-by-step plan for chairwork with a partner and relationship problem
Step 1: Establish a recurrent interaction pattern to focus on in chairwork
Step 2: Identify a Protector and its protective function in partner 1
Step 3: Identify a Protector and its protective function in partner 2
Step 4: Identify the Critical Parent and its effect on partner 1
Step 5: Identify the Critical Parent and its effect on partner 2
Step 6: Reflection on the circular processes and homework

7.5.1 Step 1: Identify a recurrent interaction pattern to focus on in chairwork

In the recurring patterns of communication and behaviour that have led to a couple seeking help, each partner is often very focused only on those aspects of the other that bother them. The advantage of chairwork is that it shifts the partners' attention from each other to the chairs.

> ### Identifying a recurrent interaction pattern – Robert and Lisa
>
> *[Robert and Lisa are in therapy because of recurring arguments. Those arguments are often about not experiencing enough appreciation from the other person. When these interactions are discussed, a similar argument ensues in the therapy room. The therapist interrupts the conversation and uses the argument as an opportunity to analyse the dynamics between the partners' different sides.]*
>
> **>>Therapist:** "Okay, Robert, listening to you, you seem to be a bit closed off just now, is that true?"
>
> **>>Robert:** "Yes, I think so too. I really have the feeling that there's no point, no matter what I say."
>
> **>>Therapist:** "Exactly. Let me try to clarify what I see happening using chairs."
>
> *[The therapist takes an extra chair and places it near Robert.]*

7.5.2 Step 2: Identify a Protector and its protective function in partner 1

Protectors play an important sustaining role in arguments between partners. With an active Protector, it is no longer possible to see the underlying emotional pain, and only behaviour that is experienced as annoying is visible. Chairs make it clear that the observable behaviour is only one side of the other person, and help to make the vulnerable, more emotional side of the other person visible.

> ### Identifying a Protector in partner 1 – Robert and Lisa
>
> >>Therapist: "Let's say that this chair is the side of Robert that I see at present, which I think is the one Lisa also sees. The Robert that is somewhat closed off. In that chair I see a Robert who no longer says much, who seems to be focusing inward a bit. Is that true, Lisa?"
>
> >>Lisa: "Yes, exactly! He doesn't say anything anymore, and that can infuriate me!"
>
> >>Therapist: "But just a moment ago, I don't think Robert felt flat or indifferent at all. I saw a very different side of him – a Robert who didn't feel appreciated or seen himself. Is that right, Robert?"
>
> >>Robert: "Yes – no matter what I do, and no matter how hard I work, none of it seems to matter. All I get is criticism!"

> >>Therapist: "Okay, okay… so even though Lisa and I just saw this closed-off side of Robert *[pointing to the empty chair that has just been placed there]*, there is still a whole other experience beyond that withdrawal. *[The therapist places an extra chair behind the first chair.]* There is also the feeling of not being seen, not being appreciated – a Vulnerable Robert. And actually, it seems like that Closed-Off Robert shuts everything out the moment the feeling of not being appreciated gets too strong. Can you both come and stand next to me, so we can look at what happens between you more deeply?"
>
> *[Robert and Lisa come to stand next to the therapist.]*
>
> >>Therapist: "And I just heard you say, Lisa, that it is very annoying to you when Robert is so closed off, is that right?"
>
> >>Lisa: "Yes, it is."

7.5.3 Step 3: Identify a Protector and its protective function in partner 2

To break through recurring arguments, more compassion for the other person is required. This applies to both partners, so it is important that chairwork also reveals the vulnerable part of partner 2 and the Protector that is guarding him or her against emotional harm.

> **Identifying a Protector in partner 2 – Robert and Lisa**
>
> >>**Therapist:** "So what I hear you saying is that you feel sad at moments like that – you don't feel seen."
>
> *[The therapist takes an extra chair and places it opposite the first two chairs].*
>
> >>**Therapist:** "Let's make this the chair for sad Lisa. But if I'm honest, I didn't see that sadness very clearly. What I saw with you in particular, Lisa, was a side of you that tries hard to make something clear to Robert – who tries to explain, sometimes in a bit of an angry way. Does that sound right?"
>
> >>**Lisa:** "Yes, sure… but then again, I can't help it – he just doesn't seem to see or get it!"
>
> >>**Therapist:** "Exactly, and then you kind of shoot into that combative state, it happens almost automatically. And that's what Robert gets to see."
>
> *[At this point, the therapist takes a fourth chair and places it in front of the vulnerable, sad part of Lisa].*
>
> >>**Therapist:** "From Robert's perspective, then, we primarily see that combative side of Lisa."

7.5.4 Step 4: Identify the Critical Parent and its effect on partner 1

You can now discuss why the behaviour of the other person's Protector has such an impact. The explanation often lies in a relationship with past pain. The other person's behaviour can activate punitive, demanding or guilt-inducing messages that the other person has experienced in their past.

> **Identifying the Critical Parent in partner 1 – Robert and Lisa**
>
> **>>Therapist:** *[now addressing Robert]* "And how do you feel then, Robert, when you see Lisa being so angry and combative, trying to make something clear to you?"
>
> **>>Robert:** "Well, then I think – I suppose I've done it all wrong again…"
>
> **>>Therapist:** "So it comes across as punitive to you?"
>
> **>>Robert:** "Yes, as if I'm not doing anything right."
>
> **>>Therapist:** *[turning towards Lisa]* "But I doubt that's what you meant?"
>
> **>>Lisa:** "No, of course not! I absolutely don't think that Robert never does anything right!"
>
> **>>Therapist:** "So, Robert does see that you're worried, but interprets it very differently from how you mean it. It's almost as if there's a translator sitting on his shoulder."
>
> *[At this, the therapist takes another chair and places it by Robert, close to Robert's Vulnerable Side].*
>
> **>>Therapist:** "And that translator gives a very different subtext to your behaviour than what you really mean, Lisa. That translator sees an angry Lisa and says to Robert: 'See, she just thinks you can't do anything right!' Because that is a message that Robert has received many times before in his life."
>
> *[Robert nods.]*
>
> **>>Therapist:** *[addressing Robert]* "That message was given to you many times in your childhood, as I understand it. And the only way to cope with that, I think, was by closing yourself off a bit, wasn't it?"
>
> *[At this, the therapist points to the chair of Robert's Protector.]*
>
> **>>Robert:** "Yes, that's pretty much right. And then a lot of the time I don't know what to say and think it's best just not to say anything at all, to avoid making things worse."

7.5.5 Step 5: Identify the Critical Parent and its effect on partner 2

Equivalence is also very important at this stage of building the two partners' mode models, to avoid identifying either one of the partners as the sole source of the problem.

> **Identifying the Critical Parent in partner 2 – Robert and Lisa**
>
> **>>Therapist:** "In his past, the best way for Robert to survive has been to retreat. But for Lisa *[turning to Lisa]*, I don't think this is the first time that people have stopped talking to you, or am I wrong?"
>
> **>>Lisa:** "No, you're not – there was never any discussion at home when I was growing up. If there was anything, it was never expressed. We all just sat silently at the table, and no one said anything."
>
> **>>Therapist:** "And how did that feel for you then, as a child?"
>
> **>>Lisa:** *[with sadness in her voice]* "As if I didn't matter; or as if I, or what I felt, wasn't important."
>
> **>>Therapist:** "So, when you see that Closed-Off Robert, you don't see his Protector – the Robert who is trying to keep his head above water so as to cope when he is sad himself. Instead, you see those silent parents at the table again, giving you the message that you aren't important?"
>
> **>>Lisa:** "Yes, I think so… it does feel like that, yes."
>
> **>>Therapist:** "Exactly, that isn't something you come up with in your head, but it feels like it. And so *[at this, the therapist places a final chair close to Lisa's sad side]* when you see that closed-off side of Robert, that translator of yours is going to run off with it. Then that Punitive Translator of yours says: 'You see, Robert isn't even interested in you, no matter what you do.' Does that sound right at all?"
>
> *[Lisa nods.]*

7.5.6 Step 6: Reflection on circular processes and homework

By taking a photo of the chairs at the end of the session, the insights can be repeated at home. Another homework assignment could be for each partner to work out their own mode model further on paper, and then to put the two mode models side by side and discuss the interactions together.

> **Reflection and homework – Robert and Lisa**
>
> **>>Therapist:** "So the problem is that you two no longer have the bigger picture when you're caught up in the heat of an argument. At such times, you *[looking at Robert]* become that Closed-Off Robert, and as soon as your Punitive Translator *[looking at Lisa]* has translated that into a very punitive message, you shoot into that Combative Protector you've had to develop in life. *[Addressing Robert again.]* On seeing that Combative Protector, your Punitive Translator immediately sees that as proof that you can never do anything right anyway and so… *[pointing at the chair of the Closed-Off Robert]* you shut down. In this way, the two of you are trapped in a vicious circle. But it's different now – we can look at it together from a distance and become aware that all this is happening. How does it feel to see it like this?"
>
> *[Robert and Lisa look together at the chairs for a while and nod.]*
>
> **>>Robert:** "Yes, this does help."
>
> **>>Lisa:** "Yes. It is a lot, but it does help to see it this way. Crazy, it's true, but I don't have any awareness of it at such moments, of those other sides…"
>
> **>>Therapist:** "Exactly, and that's why this is a first but also hugely important step – learning to recognise those different sides of each other, so you don't fall into the trap of seeing the other person's Protector as the whole person. It might also be good to take some of this home with you, as a kind of homework, to practice recognising the different parts of yourselves and each other."

In therapy, partners can learn not only to continue to see the other partner's vulnerable side, but also to support it. For instance, Robert can learn to express compassion for the sad girl that Lisa is carrying with her and let her know that he does see her and care about her feelings and needs. Lisa, in turn, can learn to have compassion for the little boy that Robert is carrying with him, who feels unappreciated. She can also learn to express the unconditional recognition and appreciation that Robert has been missing.

7.6 Group therapy

Chairwork in a group setting can be performed in the same way, in many respects, as has been described in the preceding chapters for work with individuals. All group members can participate in the exercise, making chairwork in a group setting the form that most closely resembles the original method of working with chairs in psychodrama. While one client must always be the focus of a given exercise, the other group members can take on the roles of modes or significant others, for example, so that intrapsychic or interpersonal dynamics can be re-enacted and influenced. Some examples of these group applications are described for each phase of treatment below. Note that in group schema therapy, sessions typically take place with two therapists running the group.

7.6.1 Analysis phase

Chairs can be used in the analysis phase to form a mode model (see Chapter 2). Instead of using empty chairs, other clients can be asked to play the roles of the different modes. Instructing those other group members helps the client to become more aware of the different considerations, behaviours and statements that are typical of his or her different modes.

7.6.2 Coping modes

Group members can help to reveal the effect of a Protector. For instance, the client can take a seat on the Vulnerable Child's chair. A group member then plays the Protector in a chair placed right in front of the client, with their back turned to them. One of the therapists may have a conversation with that Protector, after which the client is asked how they experienced the interaction:

- Did you feel seen during the conversation with the Protector?
- Did you feel understood when all the attention was on the Protector?
- Was it nice not to be part of the conversation, or was something missing?

Such questions can raise awareness of the benefits but also the disadvantages of a Protector. In this arrangement, you can have your client sit in the therapist's chair and converse with the Protector yourself, while another group member takes the chair of the Vulnerable Child. From this perspective, the client may come to realise that a Protector makes it impossible to contact the Vulnerable Child.

7.6.3 Parent modes

In the initial phase of therapy, it is mainly the therapist who plays an active role in fighting the Critical Parent. In group therapy, other group members can assist with this. Indeed, clients generally find it easier to stand up for another person's needs than for their own. Collectively caring for the needs of a fellow group member also contributes to the connection within the group. Group members can sit in a semi-circle in front of, or indeed behind, the client's chair while fighting the Critical Parent in the chair opposite them. Each of them can express arguments against the parent mode and, at the end of the intervention, they can collectively pick up the Critical Parent's chair and put it outside the room.

7.6.4 The Healthy Adult

Chapter 4, on the middle phase of therapy, describes how chairwork can be used to practice the three steps of the Healthy Adult. In group therapy, members of the group can play these three steps while the client sits across from them. In this approach, your client receives the healthy messages of compassion, cognitive restructuring and behavioural change directly from other members of the group. In this way, all group members benefit from the exercise. For example, group members who have difficulty expressing compassion can practice this in the chair of compassion, while other group members can learn from the exercise as observers through modelling and vicarious learning.

7.7 Grief and mourning

Around half of all those who experience the loss of a loved one recover from it without requiring professional help. 10% need clinical support. Between the two, the remaining 40% experience symptoms severe enough that preventive care is required to prevent their mental health symptoms from worsening to clinical levels (Boelen, 2020). These cases are referred to as disturbed grief.

In such cases, clients experience intense longing for a deceased person and have great difficulty accepting their loss. Longing for a deceased person and difficulty accepting the loss are a normal part of grieving, of course; however, these experiences usually diminish over time. In disturbed grief, clients become stuck in that longing for something or someone who is no longer there. Chairwork can be a good way to confront the reality of a loss, and to let go of the resistance to it. Placing the object of grief on a chair can start a dialogue – one in which the client can face up to the loss, express their feelings toward the deceased person and eventually say goodbye.

Reading a farewell letter to the deceased loved one – Nicky

>>Therapist: "We agreed last time that you would prepare a farewell letter to your late grandmother. I was wondering if we could do an exercise today to give you the opportunity to express your feelings towards her?"

[Nicky nods.]

>>Therapist: "I'll pull up another chair and I'd like you to imagine your grandmother sitting there."

[The therapist takes another chair and places it opposite Nicky.]

>>Therapist: "Imagine your grandmother sitting there in that chair. What does she look like?"

>>Nicky: "She's smiling, she has such a mischievous smile."

>>Therapist: "Okay, now could you please read the letter to her, as she sits there?"

[The therapist points to the empty chair opposite. Nicky takes the letter and starts reading aloud.]

>>Nicky: "Dear Grandma, I want to let you know what you meant to me. You were always there for me, and my life was turned upside down when you died. So I focused all my energy on work because I couldn't handle feeling that pain. I know now that this is because I didn't learn to deal with pain. My heart is broken, but I've learned that this happens to hearts sometimes. I have no idea who I will become on the other side of this loss, but I know it will be okay. All my love forever, from Nicky."

>>Therapist: "Wow… that's really very beautiful. How does it feel to read it out loud?"

>>Nicky: "Very hard…"

After reading the letter out loud, if it seems appropriate, you can ask the client to take a seat in the deceased person's chair to imagine how that other person would react to the feelings expressed. Going into the other person's perspective can help to release one's own grief and pain somewhat.

Responding as the deceased loved one – Nicky

>>Therapist: "Now I'd like to ask you to sit in Grandma's chair and respond to what you have just read out. Would you do that?"

>>Nicky: "Sure, okay."

[Nicky sits down on Grandma's chair.]

> **Therapist:** "Be Grandma now. What do you want to say, now that you've heard Nicky's letter?"
>
> **Nicky:** "I want to tell her she doesn't have to be so sad, because we had so many great times together. I want to say: 'Just keep going', or something like that."
>
> **Therapist:** "Anything else you want to add?"
>
> **Nicky:** "No, just that."
>
> **Therapist:** "Okay, then come back and sit here on the chair next to me again."
>
> *[Nicky sits down back on the original therapy chair.]*
>
> **Therapist:** "What was it like for you to sit in Grandma's chair and speak her words?"
>
> **Nicky:** "Reassuring, to find that she's still there. And I also think she really would want me to move on – she would say that I've grieved enough and it's time to get on with living my own life now."

7.8 Decision making: The Future Self

When your client is grappling with a difficult choice, chairwork can be a useful tool to help them make it. Chairs can be used to represent the different possibilities within the choice, and to express the advantages and disadvantages of each option. For example, if a client is unsure about their relationship, two chairs can be used to represent the pros and cons of choosing whether or not to break up. By looking at those chairs and the arguments they represent from the original therapy chair, the client can maintain an objective perspective and ultimately make a more considered choice.

Another possibility is to use chairs to represent your client's future self. In the Future Self's chair, your client can imagine that they are in the life that follows one of the choices. From that perspective, they can look back on the choice and the resulting life course. This allows them to have a more intense emotional experience of whether the choice is the right one, instead of simply worrying about it.

The Future Self – Greg

>>**Therapist:** "I hear how you're stuck in your doubt about whether to end your current relationship."

[The therapist takes an extra chair and places it diagonally opposite Greg.]

>>**Therapist:** "First, I'd like to ask you to sit on this chair."

[Greg sits down on the chair indicated.]

>>**Therapist:** "In this chair, I want you to imagine yourself after choosing to break up and move away from your girlfriend. Really try to imagine that this is the life you've chosen. Can you imagine it?"

>>**Greg:** "Yes, that option has been playing in my head the whole time, so it isn't difficult!"

>>**Therapist:** "Now travel forward in time, from the moment you decided to end the relationship. I want to ask you to fast forward to a point when you're old, in the last phase of your life. You're elderly, you've been retired for some years, and you feel the end is probably approaching. So, there isn't much time left to look forward to, but there's a lot to look back on. I want you to go all the way into that realisation now, that your life may be approaching its end, and, with that, you can look back on everything you've experienced in your time here on Earth. Can you imagine that?"

[Greg nods.]

>>**Therapist:** "Stay as that older version of yourself for now, and I'll speak to you as it for a moment. So, you're looking back on your life and the course it took after you decided to break off the relationship. How do you feel looking back on that now, so near the end of your life?"

>>**Greg:** "Well, I see that it was an intense time, but that after I made the choice there was peace. I felt free, though I also missed her a lot. I really enjoyed my new freedom, but looking back, I also see that we had good times together. And I was restless again, because really, I did want a relationship."

You can then ask the client to sit on a different chair and, from that chair, imagine a Future Self looking back on a life in which he chose to stay in the relationship. From the original therapy chair, both life choices can then be examined and interviewed. The aim of this is not to determine whether an option is 'right' or 'wrong'; it is simply to create distance from the doubts through the mechanism of the Future Self. With that space, it is possible to reflect on the situation more calmly, and to have a better sense of underlying needs than when the client is entangled with fears and doubts.

7.9 Chapter summary

This chapter has described a range of further applications of chairwork. Aside from a client's own sides or modes, many other things can be placed on a chair – including the desire for a substance, an automatic thought or assumption, fictitious others in a re-enacted courtroom, or another existing person when treating partner and relationship problems. A deceased loved one can also be placed on a chair and addressed in order to treat unprocessed grief, and future versions of the client can be placed on chairs in order to gain distance from and clarity concerning current doubts or struggles.

In describing these various possible applications, you have seen that chairwork lends itself well to treating many different symptoms and problems. After all, the core of the technique remains the same – the use of chairs provides the opportunity to gain some distance from an emotional experience, or from the trigger for such an experience. This distance then gives the client the opportunity to gain insights and to find more healthy ways to deal with their problems or symptoms. As such, chairwork has many different potential applications, not limited to those described sabove.

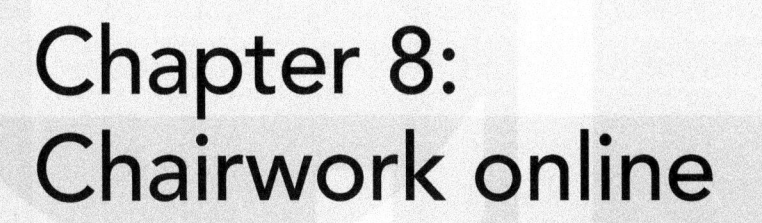

Chapter 8: Chairwork online

Chapter 8: Chairwork online

Chapter map
8.1 Introduction
8.2 General tips for online chairwork
8.3 Forms of online chairwork
8.4 Chapter summary

8.1 Introduction

Out of necessity, the amount of therapy provided online has increased dramatically in recent years. Many therapists who had no previous experience with online therapy were forced to attempt it during the COVID-19 pandemic in order to continue working, and they discovered that corrective emotional experiences could indeed be generated remotely. However, it is obviously more difficult in online therapy to use techniques that require physical movement or that make use of physical objects such as chairs. Even so, chairwork can still be used online, and this chapter will explore how to go about it. It describes various forms of online chairwork – such as movement in front of the camera, using chairs in the therapist's room, and using chairs in the client's room. First, though, it will give some general tips designed to make it easier to work with chair exercises online.

8.2 General tips for online chairwork

1. **Both therapist and client should use a laptop or tablet**
   It is strongly recommended that both you and your client have a laptop or tablet, rather than a fixed monitor screen. This makes it possible to move around the room without losing contact with each other. By

carrying a laptop or tablet as a therapist, the exercise becomes a lively experience rather than a theoretical discussion, as tends to occur when communicating through a screen. By having the client carry a laptop around, you can maintain an overview as a therapist during the exercise.

2. **Ensure that you both have enough space to work with different positions and chairs**

   Make sure that both you and your client have enough space in your respective rooms to move about and take up different positions. A very small room with one or both people wedged behind a cramped desk can make it difficult to perform chairwork exercises effectively.

3. **Ensure that the client has one or more extra chairs available**

   At the beginning of the therapy or session, check that your client has one or more extra chairs available in their room. Of course, also make sure that you have chairs available. Before the session, think about which chairs might work best for a chair exercise and, if necessary, discuss with your client how they can get an extra chair for the therapy that is light enough for them to move about.

4. **Avoid saying 'left' and 'right', instead using gestures to indicate direction**

   During the exercise, you will ask the client to take up different positions in front of the screen, with or without the use of extra chairs. Avoid talking about 'left' or 'right' when giving directions in this regard, because online connections can sometimes mirror the image on the screen. If you say: 'that chair to your left', while the client sees you on the screen gesturing to their right, this may create unnecessary confusion. Because of this, it is much easier to refer to 'that chair over there' while gesturing to the place where you want to direct your client's attention.

5. **See the camera on your laptop or tablet as the client's eyes**

   The camera on your device is not in the same place as the image of the client that you see on the screen. As a result, from the client's point of view, if you look at them on the screen you will not be looking into their eyes. For this reason, and particularly at those moments when you want to address the client directly, it is best to look straight into the camera. Your client will experience this as you looking him or her directly in the eye, which is appropriate to that moment of contact. Looking into the camera takes some effort, because your eye is likely to be drawn involuntarily to the image of your client on the screen; however, looking directly into the camera has been found to be especially important when making contact with the Vulnerable Child and the Healthy Adult. It is worth adding that for a Protector or Critical Parent, looking 'past' your client rather than looking them in the eye can sometimes actually be appropriate to the closed or self-critical state that he or she is in.

6. Use distance from the camera to regulate emotional intensity

As well as using eye contact to regulate emotional intensity, you can also use the distance between your face and the camera lens. Moving closer to the camera creates an experience of closeness, sometimes even stronger than is possible in offline therapy. As a result, and particularly when you are seeking to contact the Vulnerable Child, distance from the camera can be used as a tool to connect with your client's emotions and needs. You can emphasise this further by creating a little more distance from the camera than usual when working with a Protector or Critical Parent.

8.3 Forms of online chairwork

The recommendations above should not be taken as necessary conditions for chairwork online. Even without a laptop or extra chairs, sitting in a small room in front of a fixed computer, chair exercises that lead to corrective emotional experiences can be performed successfully. The purpose of chairwork remains to enable clients to experience more physical and emotional distance from their various sides, and this can be achieved without a lot of physical space or extra chairs.

Three forms of online chairwork are described in this section:
1. Moving in front of the camera. The therapist asks the client to move from one side of the screen to the other, in order to take up the position of a particular mode.
2. Using chairs in the therapist's room. This form of online chairwork is particularly suitable for working with the Critical Parent in the initial phase of therapy.

3. Using chairs in the client's room. This form of online chairwork is particularly suitable when working with a Protector, or when working with a Critical Parent toward the end of therapy.

8.2.1 Moving in front of the camera

This variant replaces different chairs in a room with different positions in relation to the camera. As a therapist, you can gesture to a specific side of the screen while naming a particular side of your client. In this way, that side of the screen becomes the position of the identified mode. When you want to interview that mode, you can ask the client to move that way and, as a therapist, you see the client moving in the image. Your client can also see this movement and can identify with a Protector, Critical Parent or Vulnerable Child in this new position, even without an extra chair.

> **Assigning a position in relation to the camera – Nicky**
>
> **>>Therapist:** "In your current position *[gestures to the right-hand side of the screen as well as looking at that spot]*, you seem not to feel much. I know that you *[gesturing to the camera]* can feel an awful lot. But in your current position *[gesturing once again to the right of the screen]*, that isn't the case, and you seem flat. I believe there's a reason for this. Shall we do a quick exercise to find out why?"
>
> *[Nicky nods.]*
>
> **>>Therapist:** "Okay, in that case, I now want to ask you to move a little to that side."
>
> *[The therapist gestures to the right-hand side of the screen, and Nicky moves in the direction indicated.]*

In the position indicated, you now ask the client to identify with their Protector as well as they can. You should address the Protector directly in this place using words like 'you' and 'your'. When addressing the Protector, look straight into the camera as much as possible so your client has the experience of being looked at directly, rather than seeing the therapist looking elsewhere on a screen. Being looked at directly contributes to identifying with the role of Protector.

> ### Addressing the Protector – Nicky
>
> **>>Therapist:** *[looking directly into the camera]* "In this position, I want you to be the Protector, that Non-Feeling Nicky. I believe that for you *[gestures towards the camera]*, the Protector, this feels more pleasant than if the Emotional Nicky *[gesturing to the left-hand side of the screen]* were to be there, is that right? How would she *[gesturing to the left]* feel if you *[gesturing to the camera]* were not there?"

After asking the Protector about the advantages of suppressing feelings, you can discuss the disadvantages. The discussion of these disadvantages leads to a negotiation, with the aim of making contact with your client's Vulnerable Child (see Chapter 3). If the Protector agrees, ask him or her to move to the other side of the screen. When your client is sitting in the place of the Vulnerable Child, try to support him or her as much as possible in making contact with their feelings and needs. Again, look straight into the camera while addressing the Vulnerable Child with words like 'you' and 'your'. You can intensify the emotional contact by sitting closer to the camera and speaking in a soft voice.

> ### Contacting the Vulnerable Child – Nicky
>
> **>>Therapist:** *[still speaking directly to the Protector]* "So, is it okay with you if I get the chance to help her *[points to the left-hand side of the screen]* feel better?"
>
> *[Nicky in the role of Protector nods.]*
>
> **>>Therapist:** "Then I'll take that opportunity with both hands and ask you, Nicky, to move over to that side in a moment *[pointing to the left-hand side of the screen]*. But when you do, I'd like you to leave the Protector here *[pointing at the camera]*. Leave her stuck here while you move over."
>
> *[The therapist gestures again to the left-hand side of the screen, and Nicky moves that way.]*
>
> **>>Therapist:** *[Moving a little nearer the left-hand side of the screen and closer to the camera, and speaking in a softer voice while looking straight into the camera]* "All right, here I'd like you to get in touch with all those feelings I was talking about to her *[gestures to the right-hand side of the screen]*. The Protector over there *[pointing to the right-hand side of the screen again]* said you were feeling very sad last week, and she thinks it's better not to dwell on your *[pointing to the camera]* sadness. So, you've been feeling sad – could you tell me what has made you feel that way?"

After the feelings have been explored and the needs have been validated in the form of recognition and understanding, the exercise is concluded. In an offline version of this exercise, you might now ask the client to get up and look at the chairs while standing next to you. In this standing position, the Healthy Adult side of the client is contacted, and you can share experiences and insights. In online chairwork, you can connect with the Healthy Adult by asking your client to move back a little. This relative distance makes it possible to look at the two places right in front of the camera as the places of the Protector and the Vulnerable Child. Experiences and insights are shared, and to conclude the session you give homework. This can consist of the client noting down the insights they have gained, or writing down the corrective emotional experiences that have resulted from the therapy. In online therapy, the standard audio recording of a session can be extended to a video recording of the exercise being performed. Clients who find it unpleasant to be confronted with their own image in such an audio-visual recording may choose to just listen to the audio component.

> ### Reflecting on the online chairwork exercise – Nicky
>
> **>>Therapist:** "Good, so let's now take a step back for a moment to reflect on what happened. Could you please slide your chair back a bit?"
>
> *[The therapist moves his own chair back a little, and Nicky follows suit]*
>
> **>>Therapist:** *[Now speaking to the Healthy Adult with a more rational, mature voice]* "Okay, so let's look at the two sides in front of us from a distance. There *[pointing to a place at the right-hand side of the screen, and below the camera to emphasise the new overview position]* is your Protector, who says that feeling is dangerous. She thinks it's best to suppress these feelings. But there *[pointing to a place at the left-hand side of the screen and below the camera]* is Little Nicky. She was feeling sad last week, and that sadness hasn't gone away because she *[pointing to the Protector]* is suppressing it."
>
> *[The therapist looks straight into the camera and gestures directly at it.]*
>
> **>>Therapist:** "Now be that Healthy Adult, the captain of your ship. What do you learn from this?"

8.2.2 Using chairs in the therapist's room

This variant of online chairwork is particularly useful when working with the Critical Parent in the initial phase of therapy. In this phase the Healthy Adult does not yet have a strong presence, which makes your client susceptible to the judgements of the Critical Parent. As a therapist, you are particularly needed in this phase to fight the Critical Parent and, if necessary, to remove that chair from the room. With online chairwork, you can only fight the Critical Parent through the screen – and you cannot physically remove a chair from the room if this is deemed necessary. It may still be too difficult for the client to fight and remove that chair independently at this stage, and as a result there is a high risk that the exercise will not provide the corrective emotional experience that you intend.

By using a chair in your room, you can move the Critical Parent from your client's room to your own room – and in this way you can still fight the punishing messages and take away the chair. As strange as it may sound, moving from one room to another in this way generally works well in practice without any problems. However, it is not recommended that you mention this shift to the client explicitly during the exercise, as it may draw attention to the challenges of working therapeutically online and distract from the emotional experience that the exercise should be generating.

> ### Moving the Critical Parent into the therapist's room – Nicky
>
> **>>Therapist:** "How have you felt over the past week?"
>
> **>>Nicky:** "Bad, stupid – I'm doing everything wrong and I'm a total failure."
>
> **>>Therapist:** "Okay, I'm going to interrupt you here for a moment."
>
> *[The therapist identifies the Critical Parent and asks the client to move across in front of the camera to express this self-criticism from the right-hand side of the screen. In this way, this becomes the position of the Critical Parent. You then ask the client to move back to their original position and explain how it feels to hear all that self-criticism as the Vulnerable Child.]*
>
> **>>Therapist:** "When I hear all the criticism coming from that corner *[gestures to the right-hand side of the screen]*, it's as if someone is really sitting there pouring out all that criticism about you."
>
> *[At this point, turn the camera a little to the right to reveal an empty seat next to you. This is the moment when the Critical Parent moves from your client's room to your room. However, this is not stated; it is suggested by the movement and you indicating the Critical Parent sitting next to you.]*
>
> **>>Therapist:** *[Moving closer to the camera, in the client's corner, speaking in a soft voice]* "I'm therefore wondering – who is it sitting there? Who do all those punishing messages come from?"
>
> **>>Nicky:** *[softly]* "My father…"

> **>>Therapist:** "I was thinking of him, too. So, it is actually your father sitting there *[pointing to the empty chair which is still in view]* raging at you like that. But I don't want you to have all that anger poured all over you, so I want to say something to him."
>
> *[The therapist turns towards the empty chair and challenges the imaginary father with a decisive voice.]*

Fighting these punishing messages may result in you removing the empty chair from the room. At that moment, you stand up with the laptop clasped with one hand against your upper arm or shoulder and first address again the Critical Parent in the empty chair in front of you. If you are able to keep the camera focused on this, your client will have the experience of looking over your shoulder as you stare down at the Critical Parent and speak firmly to them. Then, with your free hand, you pick up the chair and place it outside the door of your room while the client 'rides' on your shoulder.

8.2.3 Using chairs in the client's room

In the final phase of therapy, your client can learn to fight the Critical Parent using chairs in his or her own room. After identifying the Critical Parent, ask the client to choose a chair or other object in their room that can symbolise this side of them. In this exercise, you coach your client to fight the Critical Parent by themselves. For the exercise to work as well as possible, it is also important that you keep a very close eye on what is going on in the client's room. Where is the Critical Parent or Protector's chair? Where is the Vulnerable Child?

> **Using chairs in the client's room – Nicky**
>
> **>>Therapist:** "What side of you can we recognise when you speak so negatively about yourself?"
>
> **>>Nicky:** "It's that Punisher again…"
>
> **>>Therapist:** "Exactly! It's great that you can see that so clearly. Can you now choose a chair in your room to symbolise the Punisher? And let me look into your room too by turning your laptop a bit."
>
> *[Nicky takes the laptop and turns the camera so the therapist can see an empty chair.]*
>
> **>>Nicky:** "That chair there, I think…"

>>**Therapist:** "Very good! Now place that chair as close or as far away from you as matches your sense of how strong the Punisher is. If the chair is very close, it's as if he's sitting very near you. Is that how it feels? Or was it not quite that strong and is the chair fine as it is, at this distance?"

[Nicky gets up and moves the chair a little closer.]

>>**Nicky:** "Well, here then, because I did feel it strongly – that feeling as if I wasn't worth anything."

>>**Therapist:** "Very good. Now I want you to stand up to that Punisher, to tell him why he's wrong. But that means you need to bring in your Healthy Adult first. So, close your eyes and try to visualise that image of your Healthy Adult again, the captain of your ship. What can you see now?"

[If your client is able to connect with their Healthy Adult, then you can now coach them to fight the Critical Parent, and perhaps to eventually place them outside the door.]

8.4 Chapter summary

In this chapter, we have seen that it is quite possible to perform chairwork exercises online. We have given general tips for making exercises effective, such as using a laptop or tablet and getting the most from the camera. And we have explored three variants of online chairwork. The simplest is to have your client move about in front of the camera in order to assume the role of a Protector or Critical Parent. If actual chairs are used in the online exercise, you may choose to place these in your room as a therapist – this works particularly well for the initial phase of therapy when, as a therapist, you must fight the Critical Parent. Or, chairs in the client's room can be used for a Protector in the initial phase of therapy, to represent all the client's different sides in the subsequent phases of therapy, and to enable the client to fight the Critical Parent toward the end of therapy.

References

Arntz, A., Rijkeboer, M., Chan, E., et al. (2021). *Towards a reformulated theory underlying schema therapy: Position paper of an International Workgroup*. Cognitive Therapy Research.

Barnett, Jeffrey & Baker, Ellen & Elman, Nancy & Schoener, Gary. (2007). In Pursuit of Wellness: The Self-Care Imperative. *Professional Psychology: Research and Practice*. **38**. 603-612. https://doi.org/10.1037/0735-7028.38.6.603.

Beck, J. S. (1995). *Cognitive therapy: Basics and beyond*. Guilford.

Beck, A. T., Emery, G., & Greenberg, R. L. (1985). *Anxiety disorders and phobias: A cognitive perspective*. Basic Books.

Bell, T., Montague, J., Elander, J., & Gilbert, P. (2012). Multiple emotions, multiple selves: Compassion focused therapy chairwork. *The Cognitive Behaviour Therapist*, **14**, 1–17. https://doi.org/10.1017/S1754470X21000180

Bell, T., Montague, J., Elander, J., & Gilbert, P. (2020). 'Suddenly you are King Solomon': Multiplicity, transformation and integration in compassion-focused therapy chairwork. *Journal of Psychotherapy Integration*, **31**(3), 223–237. https://doi.org/10.1037/int0000240

Boelen, P. A. (2020). Persisterende complexe rouwstoornis. *Impact Magazine*, **1**.

Bögels, S. M., & Van Oppen, P. (2019). *Cognitieve therapie: Theorie en praktijk*. Bohn Stafleu van Loghum.

Clarke, K. M., & Greenberg, L. S. (1986). Differential effects of the Gestalt two-chair intervention and problem solving in resolving decisional conflict. *Journal of Counseling Psychology*, **33**, 11–15. https://doi.org/11-150022-0167186/$00.75

De Oliveira, I. R., Hemmany, C., Powell, V. B., Bonfim, T. D., Duran, E. P., Novais, N., Velasquez, M., Di Sarno, E., Alves, G. L., & Cesnik, J. A. (2012). Trial-based psychotherapy and the efficacy of trial-based thought record in changing unhelpful core beliefs and reducing self-criticism. *CNS Spectrums*, **17**, 16–23. https://doi.org/10.1017/S1092852912000399

Delavechia, T. R., Velasquez, M. L., Duran, E. P., Matsumoto, L. S., & De Oliveira, I. R. (2016). Changing negative core beliefs with trial-based thought record. *Archives of Clinical Psychiatry*, **43**, 31–33. https://doi.org/10.1590/0101-60830000000078

Goldman, R. N., Greenberg, L. S., & Angus, L. (2006). The effects of adding emotion-focused interventions to the client-centered relationship conditions in the treatment of depression. *Psychotherapy Research*, **16**, 537–549. https://doi.org/10.1080/10503300600589456

Greenberg, L. S., & Clarke, K. M. (1979). Differential effects of the two-chair experiment and empathic reflections at a conflict marker. *Journal of Counseling Psychology*, **26**, 1–8.

Greenberg, L. S., & Higgins, H. M. (1980). Effects of two-chair dialogue and focusing on conflict resolution. *Journal of Counseling Psychology*, **27**, 221-224.

Greenberg, L. S., & Malcolm, W. (2002). Resolving unfinished business: Relating process to outcome. *Journal of Consulting and Clinical Psychology*, **70**, 406–416. https://doi.org/10.1037//0022-006X.70.2.416

Greenberg, L. S., & Rice, L. N. (1981). The specific effects of a Gestalt intervention. *Psychotherapy*, **18**(1), 31–37.

Hayes, C., & Van der Wijngaart, R. (2018). *Fine tuning chair work*. www.schematherapy.nl

Kaeding, April & Sougleris, Christina & Reid, Corinne & Vreeswijk, M. & Hayes, Christopher & Dorrian, Jillian & Simpson, Susan. (2017). Professional Burnout, Early Maladaptive Schemas, and Physical Health in Clinical and Counselling Psychology Trainees. *Journal of Clinical Psychology*. **73**. https://doi.org/10.1002/jclp.22485.

References

Kellogg, S. (2015). *Transformational chairwork: Using psychotherapeutic dialogues in clinical practice*. Rowman & Littlefield.

Kramer, U., & Pascual-Leone, A. (2016). The role of maladaptive anger in self-criticism: A quasi-experimental study on emotional processes. *Counselling Psychology Quarterly*, **29**, 311–333. https://doi.org/10.1080/09515070.2015.1090395

Lang, P. J. (1979). A bio-informational theory of emotional imagery. *Psychophysiology*, **16**(6), 495–512. https://doi.org/10.1111/J.1469-8986.1979.TB01511.X

Ling, N. C. Y., Serpell, L., Burnett-Stuart, S., & Pugh, M. (2021). Interviewing anorexia: How do individuals given a diagnosis of anorexia nervosa experience voice dialogue with their eating disorder voice? A qualitative analysis. *Clinical Psychology and Psychotherapy*, **1–11**,. https://doi.org/10.1002/cpp.2652

Muntigl, P., Horvath, A. O., Chubak, L., & Angus, L. (2020). Getting to "Yes": Overcoming client reluctance to engage in chair work. *Frontiers in Psychology*, **11**, 1–16. https://doi.org/10.3389/fpsyg.2020.582856

Murphy, J., Rowell, L., McQuaid, A., Timulak, L., O'Flynn, R., & McElvaney, J. (2017). Developing a model of working with worry in emotion-focused therapy: A discovery-phase task analytic study. *Counselling and Psychotherapy Research*, **17**(1), 56–70. https://doi.org/10.1002/capr.12089

Nardone, S., Pascual-Leone, A., & Kramer, U. (2021). "Strike while the iron is hot": Increased arousal anticipates unmet needs. *Counselling Psychology*. https://doi.org/10.1080/09515070.2021.1955659

Narkiss-Guez, T., Zichor, Y. E., Guez, J., & Diamond, G. M. (2015). Intensifying attachment-related sadness and decreasing anger intensity among individuals suffering from unresolved anger: The role of relational reframe followed by empty-chair interventions. *Counselling Psychology Quarterly*, **28**, 44–56. https://doi.org/10.1080/09515070.2014.924480

Neff, K. D., Kirkpatrick, K. L., & Rude, S. S. (2012). Self-compassion and adaptive psychological functioning. *Journal of Research in Personality*, **41**, 139–154. https://doi.org/10.1016/j.jrp.2006.03.004

Paivio, S. C., & Greenberg, L. S. (1995). Resolving "unfinished business": Efficacy of experiential therapy using empty-chair dialogue. *Journal of Consulting and Clinical Psychology*, **63**, 419–425.

Pugh, M. (2020). *Cognitive behavioural chairwork*. Routledge.

Pugh, M., Bell, T., & Dixon, A. (2021a). Delivering tele-chairwork: A qualitative survey of expert therapists. *Psychotherapy Research*, **31**, 843–858. https://doi.org/10.1080/10503307.2020.1854486

Pugh, M., Bell, T., Waller, G., & Petrova, E. (2021b). Attitudes and applications of chairwork amongst CBT therapists: A preliminary survey. *The Cognitive Behaviour Therapist*, **14**, 1–12. https://doi.org/10.1017/S1754470X21000052

Robinson, A. L., McCague, E. A., & Whissel, C. (2014). "That chair work thing was great": A pilot study of group-based emotion-focused therapy for anxiety and depression. *Person-Centered & Experiential Psychotherapies*, **13**, 263–277. https://doi.org/10.1080/14779757.2014.910131

Shahar, B., Carlin, E. R., Engle, D. E., Hegde, J., Szepsenwol, O., & Arkowitz, H. (2012). A pilot investigation of emotion-focused two-chair dialogue intervention for self-criticism. *Clinical Psychology and Psychotherapy*, **19**, 496–507. https://doi.org/10.1002/cpp.762

Simionato, Gabrielle & Simpson, Susan. (2018). Personal risk factors associated with burnout among psychotherapists: A systematic review of the literature. *Journal of Clinical Psychology*. **74**. https://doi.org/10.1002/jclp.22615.

Stiegler, J. R., Molde, H., & Schanche, E. (2018a). Does an emotion-focused two-chair dialogue add to the therapeutic effect of the empathic attunement to affect? *Clinical Psychology and Psychotherapy*, **25**, 86–95. https://doi.org/10.1002/cpp.2144

Stiegler, J. R., Molde, H., & Schanche, E. (2018b). Does the two-chair dialogue intervention facilitate processing of emotions more efficiently than basic Rogerian conditions? *European Journal of Psychotherapy & Counselling*, **20**, 337–355. https://doi.org/10.1080/136425372018,1495245

Stiegler, J. R., Binder, P. E., Hjeltnes, A., Stige, S. H., & Schanche, E. (2018c). 'It's heavy, intense, horrendous and nice': Clients' experiences in two-chair dialogues. *Person-Centered & Experiential Psychotherapies*, **17**, 139–159. https://doi.org/10.1080/14779757.2018.1472138

Sutherland, O., Perakyla, A., & Elliot, R. (2014). Conversation analysis of the two-chair self-soothing task in emotion focused therapy. *Psychotherapy Research*, **24**, 738–751. https://doi.org/10.1080/10503307.2014.885146

Trachsel, M., Ferrari, L., & Grosse Holtforth, M. (2012). Resolving partnership ambivalence: A randomized controlled trial of very brief cognitive and experiential interventions with follow-up. *Canadian Journal of Counselling and Psychotherapy*, **239**, 239–258.

Van der Wijngaart, R. (2021). *Imagery Rescripting: Theory and Practice*. Pavilion Publishing and Media

Van der Wijngaart, R., & Kreutzkamp, R. (2015). *Cognitieve therapie, methoden & technieken*. www.schematherapy.nl.

Van Genderen, H., & Arntz, A. (2021). *Schematherapie bij borderline-persoonlijkheidsstoornis*. Second edition, completely revised. Uitgeverij Nieuwezijds. ISBN 9789057124853.

Van Maarschalkerweerd, F. A. T., Engelmoer, I. M., Simon, S., & Arntz, A. (2021). Addressing the punitive parent mode in schema therapy for borderline personality disorder: Short-term effects of the empty chair technique as compared to cognitive challenging. *Journal of Behavior Therapy and Experimental Psychiatry*, **73**, 101678. https://doi.org/10.1016/j.jbtep.2021.101678

Young, J. E., Klosko J. S., & Weishaar, M. E (2020 or 2005). *Schemagerichte therapie: Handboek voor therapeuten*. Bohn Stafleu van Loghum